Essential Creativity in the Classroom

Inspiring kids

Kaye Thorne

Routledge
Taylor & Francis Group

LONDON AND NEW YORK

First published 2007
by Routledge
2 Park Square, Milton Park, Abingdon, Oxon OX14 4RN

Simultaneously published in the USA and Canada
by Routledge
270 Madison Ave, New York, NY 10016

Routledge is an imprint of the Taylor & Francis Group, an informa business

© 2007 Kaye Thorne

Typeset in Galliard by
RefineCatch Limited, Bungay, Suffolk
Printed and bound in Great Britain by
Cromwell Press, Trowbridge, Wiltshire

British Library Cataloguing in Publication Data
A catalogue record for this book is available from the British Library

Library of Congress Cataloging in Publication Data
Thorne, Kaye.
Essential creativity in the classroom : inspiring kids / Kaye Thorne.
p. cm.
1. Creative thinking.   2. Blended learning.   3. Motivation in education.
I. Title.
LB1062.T46 2007
370.15'7—dc22   2006019041

ISBN10: 0–415–36880–4 (hbk)
ISBN10: 0–415–36881–2 (pbk)
ISBN10: 0–203–02906–2 (ebk)

ISBN13: 978–0–415–36880–3 (hbk)
ISBN13: 978–0–415–36881–0 (pbk)
ISBN13: 978–0–203–02906–0 (ebk)

Essential Creativity in the Classroom

'Nothing, and I mean nothing, is more important than inspiring children! If you are a teacher or parent this book, plus your enthusiasm, is all you need.'

Peter Honey, psychologist, author and management consultant

Essential Creativity is about giving **all** children the opportunity to fulfil their potential. It is about developing real partnerships between parents, teachers, businesses and the community. It is about identifying best practice, finding teachers that are inspiring and schools that are committed to providing a special learning experience. This is a book to inspire, excite and stimulate creative approaches to learning.

The book covers in detail:

*   What do you need to do to help children make the most of their creativity?
*   How do children prefer to learn? Making learning a real experience.
*   How to create an inspiring learning environment. What can teachers do to stimulate children's creativity?
*   Building self-esteem, helping individuals to believe in themselves.
*   Supporting a young person in making creative career choices.

Essential Creativity in the Classroom identifies the best ways of supporting pupils as they navigate their exciting journey through a world of learning and discovery.

Kaye Thorne is the Founder of The Inspiration Network, a highly creative consultancy, UK.

For Charlotte and Annabelle Sinclair and
Luke Thorne and children everywhere.

May you always live your dreams and make this
world a more creative and inspiring place. Don't
ever believe people who say that you can't. Just
know in your heart that you can!

Contents

Acknowledgements

I would like in these acknowledgements to pay tribute to my family, friends, colleagues, clients and fellow authors to whom I owe a great debt of gratitude for their ongoing care, support and inspiration.

I would like in particular to thank the following individuals for taking part in my research and for their ongoing support:

Alan Stanhope, former Principal, Cornwall College
Alex Machray, previous co-author
Andy Pellant, previous co-author
David Mackey, previous co-author
Deborah Moran, Independent Consultant, Epona Associates
Elizabeth Warner, The National Academy for Gifted and Talented Youth
Ed Williams, Hanover Partnership
Ian Banyard, Independent Consultant, Epona Associates
John Kenney, Independent Consultant
Kevin McGrath, Business Development Manager, Assessment & Development Consultants
Ken Sloane, The National Academy for Gifted and Talented Youth
Klaus Duetoft, Director, Irrelach Consulting Pty Limited, Australia
Llorett Kemplen, Independent Consultant, Communicashone
Mark Woodhouse, previous co-author
Mark Ridolfo, Bournemouth University
Matt Desmier, Enterprise Pavilion, Arts Institute, Bournemouth
Peter Honey, psychologist, author and management consultant
Serena Standing, Hanover Foundation

Susan Rowe, Coombes County Nursery and Infant School

All the authors mentioned in the text and 'Recommended reading' and all the staff at the CIPD and IOD libraries for their help in compiling the 'Recommended reading'

Philip Mudd and the whole team at Routledge and Colin Morgan and Richard Willis of Swales and Willis

Finally, all my very special clients and the individual creative people who took part in my various creative and 'Managing the Mavericks' surveys, including the following people who agreed to be case studies – Ben and Jonathan Finn, Will Keith, Bill Legg, Stephanie Oerton, Graham Rawlinson, Jonathan Evans and Sheena Matthews – and who ultimately have been my inspiration, my grateful thanks to you all.

Introduction

This book is not about lesson plans and how you teach creativity, but it is about how you create an environment where creativity can thrive and how you can work in a creative way to unleash the potential of your learners and yourself. It is also about connectivity, connecting parents to schools, schools to industry, schools and industry to community and one nation to another. That might seem a huge ambition, but without connectivity all we have is isolated initiatives, single stones dropped into the pool of humanity, but taken together they can create a real wave of hope and optimism.

So where do we start?

Part of this is about recognising some fundamentals. What makes a good teacher? Education is prone to experimentation and to the 'emperor's new clothes' syndrome. Long-suffering teachers are exposed to White Paper after White Paper, visits from inspectors, standards, new rules about curriculum, about-turn decisions and new initiatives, and yet intuitively many teachers know what is right. We can all give examples of the teacher who with one or two statements can make a room come alive, by showing that they are human, by smiling, by caring, by being genuinely interested in the children they teach.

It is all about engagement. Anyone who witnessed the Robbie Williams concert at Knebworth in August 2003 could not have failed to be impressed with how a diminutive figure in front of a crowd of over 125,000 on three successive nights held that audience in the palm of his hand. It was the biggest music event in British history, but, more than that, what was witnessed was an extraordinary dialogue between one man and an enormous crowd of people, some of whom had queued for hours to get in, while others waited for up to six hours to get out of the car park, and did so with great patience. Within the concert Robbie talked about his life, he had the crowd dismissing drugs, he introduced his mother from the side of the stage and he kicked off by saying 'Knebworth, for the first time in my life I am speechless. I really hope that tonight I can do a show that will make you proud.'

In the late 1970s, in coaching and youth work there was a mnemonic 'REG', which stood for 'respect, empathy and genuineness'. This has now been adopted across many disciplines, including health care and education. It's very unlikely that Williams was trained to orchestrate that audience, but what he was doing was an active demonstration of REG. Using that same intuition that the good teacher demonstrates, he knew his audience, he respected them, in turn they respected him, they listened when he spoke, he empathised with them, and they knew without a shadow of doubt that he was being genuine. In May 2006 he achieved a similar feat with Soccer Aid. This is a young man who has struggled with fame and how to manage his talent, finally finding a way of channelling his creativity for the greater good.

Schools can get a bad press, but we all remember the good teachers, those people who fostered and encouraged our embryonic talents – people who made us believe in ourselves, who saw something that perhaps even we were unaware of. These are teachers who every day demonstrate REG, who inspire others, who through their own passion, drive and commitment nurture us, encourage us to push the boundaries of our experience and pick us up and encourage us to try again when we fail. Sadly, too, we all remember the teachers who were less encouraging, who made us feel small, who ensured that we stayed silent, who made us the figure of fun, who pointed out our failings to others.

Supporting creative young people making a successful transition from school to school and ultimately to employment was one of my main motivations in writing this book. I wanted to know how we can best support the laughing and happy 3-year-old, who enters nursery school full of curiosity and questions, to successfully navigate their learning journey through education so that they emerge at 16, or 18, or later, still laughing and curious, but with their wisdom enriched by a journey of personal discovery.

Having spent many years working in vocational education I found it heartbreaking meeting young people who for many years had not been enriched or who had not even begun to understand their potential. It was equally heartbreaking coaching older people who were in mid-career, or approaching the end of their career, still carrying regrets from their early learning experiences.

What happens in our centres of learning can have enormous impact on how individuals develop. I have worked either in education or in learning and development for all of my career, and these are some of the things that I have witnessed:

- 16-year-old young people coming out from schools with little more understanding of who they are, how they learn and how to make the most of their potential than the children in the reception class that I first taught;
- talented and creative individuals marking time in corporate organisations either until they can leave and set up their own business or until they are high enough up the organisation to do something about it;
- graduates who are drifting from job to job, or taking a late gap year, because they have no idea what they really want to do, but who took any job to try to start paying back their student loan;
- adults who finally in the 'third age' of employment decided to take the risk and do what they always wanted to do; and thankfully
- some highly creative and energised young people who have received the right support, are prepared for a changing world of work and are in the right place at the right time doing the work they really want to do, working either for themselves or for organisations that have made the effort to understand creativity and talent.

I have met many inspired and committed teachers and lecturers who work exceptionally hard in creating inspiring learning environments.

The hope is that in time every child, in every school at all levels, will receive the quality of teaching that inspires them to believe in their own ability and to fully exploit their creative talent.

In an age of slogan T-shirts, perhaps we should give all children a shirt saying 'No one can make you feel inferior without your consent' (Eleanor Roosevelt) and, for teachers, 'It's never too late to be what you might have been' (George Eliot).

How to use this book

This book will explore a number of key themes:

- *Chapter 1: Daring to be different – the key to creativity and innovation.* In this chapter we explore the context for developing creativity and innovation, recognising that what schools develop industry implements, i.e. if we create generations of young people unable to think for themselves, who are not excited by new ideas, who cannot undertake whole-brain thinking, there will be no innovation.
- *Chapter 2: What's it really like to be creative?* This chapter explores creativity from a number of perspectives, first sharing some definitions of creativity, second examining some of the challenges of being creative and some of the benefits, and finally putting it into the context of either being creative yourself or working with others who are creative.
- *Chapter 3: The creativity powerhouse.* This chapter will examine the background and some of the underpinning principles of learning and how to encourage a more creative approach to learning.
- *Chapter 4: Unlocking the windows of the mind – how to create an inspiring learning environment.* The concept behind this chapter is to specifically focus on the learning experiences of young people, to identify what conditions need to be present for young people and their teachers to be most creative and, importantly, to try to release the potential that the young people could take with them from school to school and ultimately into their lives beyond formal education.
- *Chapter 5: Coaching conversations.* This chapter will focus on

how to create conversations which really engage the learner, how to encourage commitment and how to help your students create goals that are meaningful for them. Many good teachers are intuitively natural coaches, but not everyone works in this way.

- *Chapter 6: 'Rage to learn' – supporting gifted children.* In order to rediscover their creativity, people often need to relearn and unlearn some of the lessons learnt in childhood. Not everyone responds to a traditional learning environment. This chapter will explore what opportunities exist for children who are gifted and how to create environments that are more inclusive. This chapter will focus on how to support gifted individuals from a position of recognising that all children have a talent but that some may need extra support to enable them to make the most of their potential.
- *Chapter 7: Building self-esteem.* Many adults still suffer from the negative impact of their schooling; this chapter explores ways in which children can be encouraged to build inner resilience and self-belief.
- *Chapter 8: Creativity and blended learning.* This chapter highlights how blended learning can support the development of creativity and how to support creative learners through different media.
- *Chapter 9: Creativity and employment.* This chapter focuses on the links between school and work, and how to support creative young people as they make career choices. It also focuses on how to create the brand Me and how young people can follow a route to entrepreneurship.
- *Chapter 10: Fulfilling your creative potential.* This chapter is about how teachers can develop their creativity, and sources of inspiration.
- *Chapter 11: Doing it differently – how to enrich your life.* This chapter is about teachers taking time out for themselves, to achieve some of their ambitions and in doing so to provide a more stimulating learning environment for their students.
- *Chapter 12: Resources and other sources of inspiration.* This chapter together with the 'Recommended reading' identifies contacts, sources of support and sources of inspiration.

Some assumptions

The nature and scope of creativity is so broad and complex that I have had to make some assumptions about the knowledge of the reader. I am assuming that, if you are a teacher or an undergraduate reading this, you will have studied, or will be studying, some of the more detailed academic theories about thinking, creativity and how people learn. What I have tried to do within this book is to gather together current thinking about creativity, learning techniques and research with creative people to make the connections between school and employment. I have tried to make this book relevant for all teachers at all levels and so you will find references to 'learner', 'child' and 'student'. I am also conscious that the work of some writers and their concepts, tools and techniques will be very familiar to some readers, and they are only included as a point of reference in the bigger debate about creativity.

There is a logical sequence to the chapters, but experience has shown that creative people can also be unconventional, enthusiastic and risk takers. So use the book in the way that suits you and your style of learning: work through it sequentially, dip into it or start from the back!

Essential Creativity in the Classroom is unashamedly committed to the fulfilment of creative potential. Imagine if everyone was encouraged to develop their full potential, to explore the 'what ifs' in their lives, to dream the impossible dreams and, having dreamt them, to seek to achieve them. Imagine if individuals and organisations, parents and children, friends and colleagues encouraged each other and took real pleasure in each other's success. What if, instead of negative messages, we gave others and ourselves the positive messages of encouragement and success? What could the impact be on our centres of learning?

It has been hard to finish writing this book. The nature of creativity is such that we are always making new discoveries. Our curiosity about how we learn and how to create the best learning environments means that, as new technology becomes available and as our world becomes more global, we are able to share more research, talk to more people and understand more about ourselves and the children, students and learners that we work with.

As part of my ongoing research into creativity I am immensely grateful to all the gifted and talented people who have willingly shared their thoughts, ideas and passions with me. Without their contribution this book would not have been written. I hope you enjoy reading it.

> Discovery consists of seeing what everybody else has seen, and thinking what nobody else has thought.
>
> (Albert von Szent-Gyorgyi)

1 Daring to be different
The key to creativity and innovation

How creative are you? Could you enable others to be creative? Does your organization encourage creativity? Important questions in today's education environment. In this chapter we explore the context for developing creativity and innovation, recognising that what schools develop industry implements. If we create generations of young people unable to think for themselves, who are not excited by new ideas, who cannot undertake whole-brain thinking, there will be no innovation.

The generation of an innovation culture is seen as one of the most critical areas of focus for organisations in the twenty-first century. Increasingly industry is waking up to the importance of creativity and innovation. In *Business Week* (26 March 2006), Bob Sutton, author of *Weird Ideas that Work* (see 'Recommended reading') and Professor of Engineering at Stanford, states, 'The best job candidates in the future will possess a creative ability that comes from working with different kinds of people on challenging projects. If you have an MBA that's nice, but it is not enough.' In the same article, reference is made to a 2005 survey by Boston Consulting Group, stating that nearly three-quarters of their companies will increase spending on innovation, up from 64 per cent in 2004. Almost 90 per cent of the executives surveyed said that generating organic growth through innovation has become essential for success in their industry.

Yet how far is education going to meet these demands of the future? We examine the impact this has on preparing young people for employment in Chapter 9.

'Penicillin, the computer, microwave ovens and the World Wide

Web are just four examples of UK world-beating creativity that instantly spring to mind. Unfortunately, however, while these were invented here they were developed elsewhere in the world', states Nigel Crouch in *Innovation: The Key to Competitive Advantage* (2000) (see 'Recommended reading'). He continues:

> The UK's track record for successfully exploiting ideas and turning them into highly lucrative UK innovations is appalling. How then do we bridge the gap between inspired invention and fully fledged innovation? Encouragingly, the answer lies very close to home with a number of British Millennium Product companies, who have contributed to the Living Innovation programme being run by the Future and Innovation Unit of the DTI in conjunction with the Design Council. This takes a look behind the innovation processes at work over a broad cross-section of Millennium Products and has generated some rich pointers as to how to innovate more effectively.

The report states that the essence of successful innovation came down to three key elements:

- unique understanding of customers and markets;
- an outstanding ability to implement;
- inspirational and cultural leadership.

It added that it was essential that a company gets all of them right in order to make a critical difference to the bottom line.

However, there would be no innovation if creative ideas were not generated in the first place. Equally, identifying how to innovate successfully is only one of the steps in a very long pipeline to become world-class innovators. The very first steps towards this are taken in schools with the development and fostering of creative thinking and understanding of how to generate creative ideas. Tony Buzan in *Head Strong* (2001) (see 'Recommended reading') states that creative ideas need to be 'original, removed from the norm and as such, they are usually exciting'.

Professor Stephen Heppell, in the introduction to the *Create and Motivate Education Guardian Supplement: Using Technology to*

Encourage Creativity in Class (7 March 2006) explains his surprise at the lack of mention of creativity in a recent government White Paper, 'Higher Standards, Better Schools for All' (October 2005):

> How many mentions does the word get in 'Higher Standards, Better Schools for All' (October 2005) White Paper? 'Standard' is mentioned 144 times, 'Fail' appears 53 times. Rather surprisingly the words 'creativity' and 'creative' are not mentioned at all, probably unique for an education policy paper in the 21st century. But where the White Paper has failed spectacularly to notice creativity, our teachers, students and parents are embracing it, armed with some very useful new tools. All around the UK schools are seeing remarkable levels of engagement and effort resulting from a quite specific focus on creative activity.

Later in the same supplement, Julie Nightingale quotes Alan Rodgers, primary representative at the education technology advisers organisation Naace, 'People are beginning to have confidence in creative activities rather than sticking rigidly to the QCA schemes of work', and Mark Rogers, MD of Apple UK, Ireland and Nordic regions, 'The creativity path is a much better option for a lot of pupils, which doesn't mean that only certain types of pupils should have access to creative activities in the curriculum. It actually means a different way of doing things for everyone.'

Equally some credence should be given to the findings from the Ofsted report *Expecting the Unexpected: Developing Creativity in Primary and Secondary Schools* (August 2003):

Overall inspectors found:

- head teachers placed the development of creativity high on their list of priorities in the majority of schools visited;
- the schools that promoted creativity effectively were outward looking, welcoming and open to ideas from external agencies;
- children's creativity was not associated with radical new teaching methods, but the willingness of teachers to observe, listen and work closely with children to help them develop their ideas in a purposeful way. Exemplifying this was a

primary school teacher who told her class, 'the unexpected is expected in my lessons'.

However, if we take an overview of the path from the incubation of an idea through to its successful implementation there is still some way to go before all schools, primary and secondary, further and higher education, and organizations embrace the importance of creativity and innovation and develop it in a fully joined-up manner. So just how do you encourage creativity and innovation? First let's focus on innovation.

Innovation

One of the most overused words in corporate communications is 'innovation'. It is found in mission and value statements, in employee competencies and inevitably in recruitment advertisements. However, the desire to acquire it often outweighs the understanding of exactly how to achieve it. Ask any CEO their view on innovation and they will all agree that it is important. If you subsequently ask them what they are doing about it their response is more guarded. The real issue is that, although everyone wants it, they really are not sure how to go about achieving it.

There can also be a lot of 'hype' about 'innovative' organisations and a common belief that you need a leader like Branson, Dyson or Gates. In reality it is within the corporate capability of any organisation to foster and develop innovation. Equally, creating a culture of innovation is as relevant to education as it is to a larger corporate organisation.

Being innovative in education can be seen as a challenge for some schools as they may feel that increasing external pressure has robbed them of their opportunity to be innovative. Faced with increasing testing, reporting and the National Curriculum they may question the opportunity to be innovative. However, schools like the Coombes School (see Chapter 4) positively relish the opportunity to be innovative almost in spite of the National Curriculum. It is much more about creating the right environment and really seeing challenges as opportunities.

It is not about investing vast resources. What is required is a real understanding of how innovation works and a commitment to create an environment which not only encourages idea generation but also has a process to follow it through. Really successful organisations do not simply innovate; they accelerate and innovate again.

Supporting creativity and innovation

Creative people are often viewed as being 'difficult' to manage; innovative organisations are perceived as being unusual, with a certain level of 'wackiness'. As a result, many organisations have reservations about their capability to accommodate these differences.

Tom Peters, in his book *The Circle of Innovation* (1997), gives some examples of these viewpoints when he reproduces the following quotes from different writers:

> Our most beloved products were developed by hunch, guesswork, and fanaticism, by creators who were eccentric – or even stark raving mad.
>
> (Jack Mingo, author of *How the Cadillac Got its Fins*)

> You say you don't want emotional, volatile, and unpredictable, just imaginative? Sorry, they only come in a package . . . I can offer you a dedicated, loyal, honest, realistic, knowledgeable package, but the imagination bit would be rather limited.
>
> (Patricia Pitcher, author of *The Drama of Leadership*)

Daniel Goleman, in his book *Working with Emotional Intelligence* (1998), describes it as follows:

> The creative mind is by its very nature a bit unruly. There is a natural tension between orderly self-control and innovative urge. It's not that people who are creative are out-of-control emotionally; rather, they are willing to entertain a wider range of impulse and action than do less adventurous spirits. That is after all what creates new possibilities.

Starting from an early age, these creative individuals may also have had a lifetime of asking questions, or making suggestions which may have been largely ignored, or dismissed as being too fanciful, or impractical, or too difficult to answer. The reasons for this are many. The ability to be creative and to generate innovative ideas has often been perceived as something outside the normal realm of behaviour, and in many ways creative people often suffer for their craft before they gain recognition.

The really innovative organisations, however, are those where creativity and innovation are recognised and encouraged, not just in a special group of people called 'Creatives', but where everyone is involved in the 'good idea' philosophy.

Creating the 'right' environment can be more of challenge. Lack of understanding about the process of innovation has traditionally led to people dividing themselves into two camps: those who are seen as creative and those who are not. This applies to individuals' assessment of themselves as well as the perception of others. By recognising how the process of innovation works, individuals and teams can develop a clearer understanding of and respect for each other's contribution.

Managing the process of innovation is absolutely critical for its success. Starting in schools, understanding how ideas are generated, sponsoring creative thinkers and allowing people freedom to think are an important part of the role of any teacher. The really excellent schools are those that assemble teams where creative and innovative people are supported by others who can help them explore their ideas and people who can help them take an idea to the next stage of making it happen. Within this environment, high trust develops, allowing ideas to be challenged, modified and implemented while remaining true to the original concept, thus enabling the creative and innovative people to move on to generating the next good idea.

If you want to assess your school's ability to foster innovation, you may like to find answers to the following questions:

- Is there top management support? Does the head and the board of governors sponsor innovation and creativity?
- Do we as a team of teachers champion idea generation?
- Do we accept ideas that break organisational precedent?

- Do we encourage cross-fertilisation of ideas and perspective?
- Do we give children, young people and teachers personal space to be creative?
- Do we tolerate failure in the pursuit of a good idea?
- Are changes in direction accepted as necessary?
- Do we reward ideas that develop the success of our school?

Characteristics of creative and innovative organisations

Creative and innovative organisations:

- nurture creativity;
- are supportive but challenging;
- develop effective teamwork;
- encourage cross-school communication and coordination;
- build networks;
- support innovation;
- recognise small changes;
- allow time for reflection and debate;
- encourage active participation and involvement;
- create a climate of cooperation and trust.

Retaining good teachers is critical in today's buoyant economic environment; every head teacher needs to identify why their good teachers would want to stay with them.

So how do schools sponsor innovation and creativity?

1 Create an environment where good ideas are the philosophy of the whole school rather than in the minds of a few creative people. Develop the 'spirit of enterprise'.
2 Recognise the innovation process and encourage staff teams and children to work together building on each other's strengths.
3 Encourage one or two individuals to take a proactive approach to idea generation.
4 Suspend overly critical judgement; instead, give evaluative and positive feedback to help the idea generator explore options

and choices for implementation. Far too many good ideas are lost because of overly critical judgement applied too soon.

5   Develop values of trust, integrity and freedom of spirit.

6   Encourage a climate of self-awareness; create a learning environment where individuals are encouraged to identify their preferences when innovating.

7   Play to individual strengths within a team, not expecting those who generate an idea to implement it. Create strong communication and feedback channels to ensure that the original concept is maintained.

8   Build networks with parents and the community, and in the broader global education marketplace. Develop zones of creativity.

9   Invite creative people with a whole range of talents into the school. Build children's knowledge of different creative careers.

10   Create a coaching environment where teaching colleagues are encouraged to share learning and where knowledge and wisdom are valued.

11   Streamline processes for evaluation, decision making and feedback, thus increasing speed to implementation.

12   Champion individuals who think differently. Share your best practice. Seek to be the school that others benchmark against.

As we move further into the twenty-first century, the need to continuously innovate will become even more important and the need to retain talent will continue to be critical. However, there will be no real progress if we retain the status quo. In the words of Ridderstråle and Nordstrom in *Funky Business* (2000):

> To succeed we must stop being so goddam normal. If we behave like all the others, we will see the same things, come up with similar ideas and develop identical products and services. At its best, normal output will produce normal results. In a winner takes all world, normal = nothing. But, if we are willing to take one little risk, break one tiny rule, disregard a few of the norms, there is at least a theoretical chance that we will come up with something different, actually get a niche, create a short term monopoly, and make a little money. Funky business is like playing the lottery. If

you participate there is a 99% chance that you will lose. On the other hand if you do not take part, your chances of losing are 100%.

This quote may have originated in the business world, but it has just as much relevance to the world of education, not just in the development of excellent schools but in preparing young people to move beyond school to the world of work.

2   What's it really like to be creative?

You need chaos in your soul to give birth to a dancing star . . .

(Nietzsche)

This chapter explores creativity from a number of perspectives, first sharing some definitions of creativity, second examining some of the challenges of being creative and some of the benefits and finally putting it into the context of either being creative yourself or working with others who are creative.

What is creativity?

One dictionary definition is 'Inventive and imaginative, creating, or able to create' (*Concise Oxford Dictionary*, 9th edition). While accurate, none of these words sums up what it means to me or the creative people that I have worked with.

Creativity to me means mess, freedom, jumbled thoughts, words and deeds each fighting to claim their own space in my mind, and deciding, given even small amounts of free time, whether I shall write, paint, draw, take off to the beach with a camera, run outside, turn my house upside down to create a new environment, plant a garden or plan a new business. Or in a more formal sense it is the original thought, the spark, the ignition, the original design concepts or the blueprint.

If we look at the great creative people of our time, we will identify a number of other distinguishing features:

- a level of pain and anguish that many people have suffered for their art;
- lack of recognition – many people's talents are not recognised until after their death;
- that, while some die young, others are late developers and many do not achieve their best work until late in life;
- an unconventional lifestyle or ideas – many do not fit comfortably into society;
- blinding self-belief – they just know they are right, even if no one else believes them;
- equally huge self-doubt – never believing that their work is good enough.

The creative mind can be a rare gift, or a huge challenge.

You cannot really legislate for creativity. It is very similar to innovation. Many organisations claim to want it, but the most that people can do is to create the environment and the support to nurture it. However much you might like to access it, so much depends on the individual's willingness and ability to share it, particularly if they have a history of sharing some of their most precious jewels in the past and others not valuing them enough or ridiculing them.

But, without creativity, we have no real innovation; we need people who are pure idea generators and we need others who can modify those ideas. We need people who learn from others' mistakes. We need people who instead of asking 'Why?', ask 'Why not?' or 'What if . . . ?' We need people who are capable of thinking crazy, out-of-the-box thoughts; we need people who shake us out of complacency.

However we try to disguise it, people who are creative are different. In my research with people who described themselves as 'mavericks' (Thorne, 2003 – see 'Recommended reading') there was a clear recognition of the implications of their overwhelming need to do things differently. It is often difficult to apply order to creativity; these individuals have also had a lifetime of asking questions or making suggestions that may have been largely ignored or dismissed as being too fanciful, impractical or difficult to answer.

The reasons for this are many. The ability to be creative and to generate innovative ideas has often been perceived as something outside the normal realm of behaviour. Inventors like Trevor Baylis (of clockwork radio fame), James Dyson (vacuum cleaners) and Steve Jobs of Apple and Pixar are often viewed with a mixture of awe and scepticism, and in many ways creative people often suffer for their craft before they gain recognition, particularly if they challenge assumptions or the status quo.

Generating ideas and being innovative take tremendous personal discipline; every person who is creative lives with the pressure of days when their mind is a complete blank, and they often have the additional pressure of knowing that someone else is waiting for them to come up with original thoughts. This applies in education as well as business: the teacher who each year comes up with a production for Christmas, the summer festival and the latest fund-raising idea; and the individual teacher who intuitively knows that there is a better way of doing things and who will find a way around the constraints of the curriculum, or a solution to the perennial 'We're bored, miss. Can we do something different?'

Equally, they know that, when they leave work and are at home at night, they may suddenly find their mind racing with the solution to the problem they have been wrestling with all day. It works the other way too, when people finally leave their place of work knowing that outside they can pursue the ideas that have been burning away inside them all day. It's not all bad news: many working in education and learning and development would say that this environment presents people with more opportunities than most to be creative. What frustrates teachers is when they see this opportunity being diminished, when intuitively creative teachers, who love stimulating young people's imaginations, find themselves spending more and more time dealing with paperwork or preparing people for tests.

Recognising that people are different and allowing people to take time out to think or to create their own personal space are essential for the development of creativity. Often it only takes a small adjustment in the management process to allow the degree of flexibility that creative people crave. Having the head teacher understanding and supporting the process of innovation and creativity is absolutely critical for its success.

Understanding how ideas are generated, sponsoring creative thinkers and allowing people the freedom to think are important parts of the role of any head. This support also needs to include opportunities for real and constructive feedback. The process has to include testing and piloting to identify what works, what needs modification and what may need further research. The really excellent head teachers are those who assemble teams where creative and innovative people are supported by others who can help them explore their ideas and can help them take the ideas to the next stage of making them happen.

Within this environment high trust develops, allowing ideas to be challenged, modified and implemented while remaining true to the original concept, thus enabling the creative and innovative people to move on to generating the next good idea.

As part of the background research to this book and others, individuals were asked what was the hardest part of being creative. The following section shows some of their responses.

What is the hardest part of being creative?

Definitely putting ideas into actions. I get bored quickly and find myself wandering from the tasks at hand. No self-discipline, I guess!

Too many ideas, not enough time.

Creative block probably.

Coming up with the initial ideas. Also I find it difficult to 'create' around something that I personally have little or no interest in.

The hardest part is crafting and finishing up ideas. Sometimes I feel that anyone can have an idea, but it is in implementing it that you really understand it properly. Finding time to implement ideas is hard.

Never believing that I am done or that it is good enough . . . Always seeing another path to go down.

Other people not seeing the picture, putting the details around the vision to make it happen.

Doing it to order? Getting others to buy in? Realising that my idea is not necessarily the best?

Convincing others to see, believe and go for the opportunity that exists.

In convincing others about the utility of my ideas. Sometimes, I don't care.

I'm not sure I can answer this question, as I enjoy everything about being creative. Lying awake at night with ideas I treat as a gift, even if I'm not sure how I will use the ideas. I enjoy others calling me to pick my brains.

If I am honest, I guess the most frustrating feeling is that at some time others will get the idea too, even though I had it first. So I guess I like to be the first and the only. Once everyone is doing it I feel disappointed and want to find something else. Also I have a very vivid imagination, so staying in atmospheric hotels is very difficult – seriously, it has become almost impossible for me to sleep and this is definitely a bad thing.

Finding employers and colleagues who really demand and can digest the creative, non-conventional. Most people seek safety and familiarity.

Getting started with a blank sheet of paper on something outside of my own experience.

Knowing when it's not appropriate!

Getting others to see what's inside your head and appreciate it.

Knowing when to let well alone.

When you have no ideas and trying too hard to make it happen.

Lacking resources. Fighting for resources. Coping with conflict from change. Resistant colleagues. Dismissive behaviour.

Being ahead of others and them not seeing the point.

Others who are blockers, with no/limited vision, often lazy.

Being a prophet in my own land.

Maintaining the energy levels in the face of opposition.

What is the most rewarding part of being creative?

Creative people are sometimes accused of not having staying power. What is interesting is that many of the respondents cited seeing their ideas coming to fruition, or implementation, as one of the most important parts of being creative. A number of people mentioned the 'buzz', the energy, excitement and ultimately the pride of being involved in the creative process. For others it was important to be 'first', or different, and they mentioned the disappointment when others caught up, prompting them to want to discover something else that was new. Here is a selection of the responses:

Seeing your creations in use!

Seeing ideas coming into fruition and getting results. Solving problems and getting results using different approaches. Getting people to think differently. I love the Eureka! moments when people's lights come on. I get a real buzz from this.

Seeing things through to a conclusion – getting feedback that these ideas are 'good'.

Seeing an elegant product/solution and having the appreciation of one's peers/colleagues.

The buzz of achieving a breakthrough that makes others go 'Great!' Then seeing it become real.

The fun of having an idea is good, but the real reward is when you see what you have created, whether it's in the garden or something you have published at work.

Success – goals achieved in a brilliant and simple way.

The people I get to work with.

Being able to create the world that I want to live in. Some of it isn't there yet but I'm working on it. It's all about the Henry Ford quote – 'Whether you think you can or think you can't you're absolutely right.'

Proving the doubters wrong; solving 'the problem' and seeing a result (but not necessarily the one I thought of!).

Success. Knowing that you achieved something that was better and different to conventional paths.

The sensation when everything becomes clear and you have developed a concept (light bulb turns on).

Finding your true self and changing the programming.

Delivering on the promise of the concept.

Success, the fact that you, the team or the business succeeded in doing something that others didn't, couldn't or wouldn't see.

Being different – if only for a while! Seeing connections before others.

Being praised for being creative is a motivation for me – as I was never good at drawing at school! We now know that that doesn't mean that you are not creative but even now I would like to be able to draw and paint more than any other skill. So I guess getting some form of credit for being creative at all is a wonder to me.

Standing out.

'Ownership' of an idea.

Originality.

Seeing something new and different take shape.

Sense of personal satisfaction, when others get excited about a creative idea of mine.

Creation and connection with others and the moment.

The fun, and the difference, and the unusual, and the feeling of reward that you get . . . and indeed PRIDE.

What do you need to do to help children make the most of their creativity?

The rest of this book is really about this, but what is interesting is that if you look at the responses above from adults you begin to get an insight into what drives creative children. In Chapter 6 we explore in more detail gifted children, but gifted children may or may not be creative in quite the same way as these adults. Creativity can be more difficult to classify and measure.

With some children you may never get to the inside of their creativity, for they do not know how to let you in. For a variety of reasons they do not understand the power of what lies within them. They know they can create imaginary friends and places. They know they love daydreaming and just occasionally they share some of their thoughts with you in their writing or drawings. However, as we see in Chapter 6, their thoughts may be so in advance of those of their peers that being open about their thoughts often brings ridicule and so gradually they withdraw into their own world.

They can be very ambitious with their thoughts; many of today's entrepreneurs had their first business ideas in the playground. I started to write a novel when I was 11 and commissioned my best friend to do the illustrations, until my parents intervened and said that homework was much more important. My son, however, with encouragement had his first novel published at 22. As we see from the comments above, implementation is one of the hardest things for creative people. The energy required to get an idea accepted often means that they lose interest once they use up their initial enthusiasm. Also, for many, they have so many ideas that they genuinely do not know what to do with them. They also may have unusual sleep patterns because they have nightmares, or waking time at night when they read, write or just dream in a form of extended daydream. Because of this their minds may also drift at school. Sometimes, too, they just want to withdraw into their own world because their thinking exhausts them, as they often exist in a kind of dual world, appearing to be absorbed in what is being said to them, when in reality their minds are somewhere completely different.

What do you need to do to make the most of your creativity?

This is covered in more detail in Chapters 10 and 11, but here is a checklist of ideas to be thinking about:

1   Recognise it, embrace it and give as much time to it as possible.

2 The more you practise, the better you get. Experiment with different ideas and different media. Some will work; others won't. Don't be afraid to give up on an idea or a creation. Do the best you can and then move on.

3 Being creative in one field does not make you creative in all fields. Some people just have great ideas, but that in itself has huge potential.

4 Go with the 'flow'. When you are having your best ideas, try to capture them as fast as you can. Just make quick notes, mind-map and use any material – napkins, menus, scraps of paper, anything – to capture your thoughts.

5 If you are *trying* to be creative, it probably won't work. Go and do something else and the thoughts are more likely to pop into your head.

6 Try to help other people understand that you will need time on your own. Being creative is often a solitary occupation. If you prepare your friends and family, they are more likely to be there for you when you need them!

7 Take time to indulge your senses, visit centres of culture, look at other artists at work, embrace your creativity and network with others in your preferred area of interest.

8 Recognise that you are your own worst critic. Share your efforts with trusted people first, and recognise that not everyone will 'get it'.

9 Creativity is not age driven. You have it when you are born and it stays with you throughout your life. You can ignore it, but it won't go away.

10 Creativity rarely comes in a neat package. It can be chaotic and disorderly. It also has no sense of timing; it arrives when you least expect it.

11 Being creative can be exhausting. In many ways you never finish. Just when you think you have, another thought or another way of doing things occurs to you. Eventually you have to stop. This is why artists, filmmakers, musicians and writers create sequels.

12 Make decisions about how you want to use your creativity. If you want to make money from it, the chances are you will need support from someone else, to help you fully maximise its

potential. If you just want to use it to enrich your life or the lives of others, it will be easier.

13 If you believe that you have created something unique or have a unique idea, protect it, but recognise that the path to commercial success may be a long and hard one.

14 Enjoy it. Recognise that creativity can be found by doing almost anything. You do not have to be a great artist, writer or musician. It's about idea generation, putting things together in combinations that no one has seen before and being original.

The most important thing is to start . . .

Whatever you think you can do or believe you can do, begin it. Action has magic, grace and power in it.

(Johann von Goethe)

3   The creativity powerhouse

All you need to do to become the artist, scientist and architect of your cathedrals of Thought, Creativity and Memory, is to apply your own brilliant conglomeration of brain cells to the manufacture of their own increasing sophistication, power and brilliance.

(Tony Buzan, *Head Strong*, 2001)

Developing creativity

Often people shy away from discussing creativity because they do not really understand it. This chapter will examine the background and some of the underpinning principles of learning and how to encourage a more creative approach to learning.

We know through the work of E. Paul Torrance, David Kolb, Honey and Mumford, Daniel Goleman and Howard Gardner that people respond positively to different learning stimuli; but despite progress there is still much work to do to help organisations, whether they are schools, further or higher education establishments or places of employment, become somewhere that individuals enthusiastically want to attend.

Below is a summary of some of the key theories behind how people learn. It is very likely that you will already be familiar with a number of them and, if so, I apologise for including them again. However, what is important is that taken together they provide a very useful blueprint for engaging with all learners and stimulating creativity.

Making learning a real experience

You've only got to watch a group of schoolchildren, particularly secondary students, on the way to school to recognise that sadly education is rarely seen as something to enjoy or to be stimulated by. Talk to a group of teenagers trying to decide what qualifications to take or trying to select a career and it very quickly becomes apparent that, for most, school is a place they go because they must, rather than because they want.

Equally, many adults equate learning with experiences that they would rather forget; therefore awakening the learning giant within is a real challenge, but also a fantastic opportunity. There is a lot of focus on the phrase 'lifelong learning', but to achieve it takes far more than the setting up of government initiatives. It means enabling people to understand, explore and then take ownership of the learning that really matters for them. The very nature of this approach has to mean that the 'one size fits all' approach really doesn't work, just as the misshapen T-shirt with the label 'one size' cannot compare to the unique tailoring and fit of a made-to-measure garment. Learning that means something important, personal and special to the individual will have far more impact than a generic learning product. So how can we apply this principle to developing creativity in all children whatever their age?

How do children prefer to learn?

Many children prefer to learn through doing or, as Kolb might describe it, 'active experimentation' (see page 29). Some prefer conversations with another person as a sounding board or with someone who is like-minded who can help them explore their ideas further, adding to their picture or reshaping certain aspects of it. This also reflects the way that many children prefer to learn, discovering with others rather than being told the facts by a specialist. What is important is the need for feedback. Even though individuals may want to learn through discovery, they also want to know how well they are doing and to have access to support when they need it.

Learning is one of the most individual and personal activities that we ever undertake and yet most of us spend most of our learning lumped together in learning environments which give us very little opportunity for individual coaching and support. For creative and innovative people, whatever their age, this is even harder. They crave feedback; they need time to reflect; they want very specific coaching to help them develop what they know they need to know. Unlike many others they often have a purpose to their learning and they get incredibly frustrated with what they may perceive as trivia or irrelevant information. This is covered more in Chapter 6.

One of the most enduring models about learning is Kolb's learning cycle; he identified the key steps in how people learn. He defined those steps as follows:

- *Having an experience*, which essentially means 'doing' something. Searching out new and challenging experiences, problems and opportunities. Finding like-minded people to learn with. Making mistakes and having fun.
- *Reviewing the experience* and reflecting on what went well and what could have been improved, as well as seeking feedback from others. Standing back from events to watch, listen and think. Listening to a wide cross-section of people with varying views. Investigating by probing, assembling and analysing information. Reviewing what has happened, and what you have learnt.
- *Theorising about what happened and why, and then exploring options and alternatives.* Questioning and probing logic and assumptions. Exploring ideas, concepts, theories, systems and models. Exploring interrelationships between ideas, events and situations. Formulating your own theories or models.
- *Planning what to do differently next time.* Sharing best practice and seeing how others have done it. Looking for practical applications of ideas. Finding opportunities to implement or teach what you learn. Trying out and practising techniques with coaching and feedback.

It is important to recognise that not all learning takes place in a neat and ordered way. We learn best when we combine all four approaches to learning:

- theory input;
- practical experience;
- application of theory;
- idea generation.

Kolb's learning cycle is also linked to the work of Honey and Mumford and their Learning Styles Questionnaire.

We all prefer to learn in slightly different ways:

- Activists learn best by doing.
- Reflectors learn best by observing.
- Theorists learn best by thinking things through in a logical and systematic manner.
- Pragmatists like to learn through putting their ideas into practice and testing them out.

To find out more detail about your or your learner's preferred learning style you may wish to undertake the Honey and Mumford Learning Styles Questionnaire (www.peterhoney.com). The definitions below give you some examples of the different types of learning style. Try to identify which of the learning styles appeals to you or the person you are working with.

Activists:
- enjoy new experiences and opportunities from which they can learn;
- often do things first and think about them later;
- enjoy being involved, are happy to be in the limelight and prefer to be active rather than sitting and listening;
- often look for new challenges;
- like to learn with people who are like-minded;
- are willing to make mistakes;
- like to have fun when they are learning.

Reflectors:
- prefer to stand back from events, to watch and absorb information before starting;
- like to hear other people's viewpoints;

- like to review what has happened and what they have learnt;
- prefer to reach decisions in their own time;
- do not like to feel under pressure.

Theorists:
- like to explore methodically, think problems through in a step-by-step logical way and ask questions;
- can be detached and analytical;
- like to be intellectually stretched and may feel uncomfortable with lateral thinking, preferring models and systems;
- prefer to come up with their own theories or models.

Pragmatists:
- like practical solutions and want to get on and try things;
- dislike too much theory;
- sometimes like to find out how the experts do it;
- like to experiment and search out new ideas that they want to try out;
- tend to act quickly and confidently;
- are very down-to-earth and respond to problems as a challenge.

An individual may find that they have a preference for one or two learning styles, or they may find that, like a small percentage of people, they have a balanced learning style. Kolb's ideas about learning and Honey and Munford's learning styles link well together. They also link with the following model of how people learn something new:

- *Unconscious incompetence:* 'I don't know what I don't know and I don't know that I don't know it.' Ignorance is bliss!
- *Conscious incompetence:* 'I know there are things that I should know, but I am not able to do them yet.'
- *Conscious competence:* 'I know what I should know and how to use my knowledge to put it effectively into practice.'
- *Unconscious competence:* 'I now do things without consciously thinking about how I do them.'

Using the whole brain

As well as understanding their learning style, students will also have a preferred way of operating through their left or their right brain. The research of Sperry and Onstein showed that we have two hemispheres in our brain, which have different characteristics or functions:

Left brain	*Right brain*
Logic	Rhythm
Lists	Colour
Linear	Imagination
Words	Daydreaming
Numbers	Intuition
Sequence	Spatial awareness
Analysis	Music

If you have always primarily used one side of your brain, you may find it harder to use the other. You may believe that you are no good at a particular subject, e.g. you may say 'I am no good at maths' or 'I've never been able to draw.' However, researchers like Tony Buzan (Buzan@mind-map.com), who developed the Mind Maps® technique, are showing that we need not be totally left-brained or right-brained, but that by using both sides of our brain in our activities we become more 'whole-brained'.

Mind Mapping® is a powerful way of expressing thoughts which has enormous value and relevance for both teachers and children alike. It is a lifelong tool. The basic technique is to combine lines, text and images to represent related ideas and concepts. The technique can be used in a variety of contexts, including note taking, summaries of visits, problem solving, decision making, planning and designing learning, life planning and career choices, etc. Buzan emphasises the importance of seeing Mind Maps® as a whole-brain activity. One of the great advantages of Mind Maps® is that large amounts of information can be summarised on one page, and from the initial map project plans can be created. Further information is available through www.mind-map.com. Another technique is de Bono's Six Thinking Hats. With Six Thinking Hats, Edward de Bono shows how to maximise your own mind's effectiveness and help groups work creatively together. He uses a technique to separate thinking into different types. For further information, contact www.Edwdebono.com.

One of the most interesting developments in learning has been the work of Howard Gardner. Searching for an alternative view to that of intelligence as a single entity, in *Frames of Mind* (see 'Recommended reading') Gardner outlined a theory of 'multiple intelligences'. In the context of developing creativity, Gardner's work is like presenting teachers and children alike with a key to unlock their understanding about how they learn and how best to learn. Gardner suggests that, while we all possess to some degree the full range of intelligences, individuals differ in the particular profiles of strengths and weaknesses that they exhibit. In *Extraordinary Minds* (1997), Gardner suggests:

> These differences make life more interesting, but they also complicate the job of school; if we all have different kinds of minds, then it is simply inappropriate to teach us all as if our minds were simple variations along a solitary bell curve. Indeed each of us should pay scrupulous attention to what is special in our own minds as well as the minds of the children over whom we have responsibility.

Multiple intelligences

Howard Gardner argued that everybody possesses at least seven measurable intelligences, which he defined as follows:

1 *Linguistic intelligence* – the intelligence of words. These people like to read and write, and play word games. They are good at spelling, and verbal and written communication. They like learning from books, tapes, lectures and presentations.

2 *Logical–mathematical intelligence* – the intelligence of logic and numbers. They like experimenting with things in an orderly and controlled manner, organising tasks into sequence and solving problems. They learn by creating and solving problems and playing mathematical games.

3   *Musical intelligence* – the intelligence of rhythm, music and lyrics. They may play musical instruments, often sing or hum to themselves, and like relaxing to music. They learn by using music and may use rhymes to help them remember things.

4   *Spatial intelligence* – the intelligence of mental pictures and images. They think and remember in pictures, and like drawing, painting and sculpting. They use symbols, doodles, diagrams and Mind Maps® to learn.

5   *Bodily–kinaesthetic intelligence* – the intelligence of expression through physical activities. They are good with their hands, and like physical activity, sports, games, drama and dancing. They learn through doing, taking action and writing notes. They need frequent breaks when learning.

6   *Interpersonal intelligence* – the intelligence of communicating with others. These are people who are good with others. They know how to organise, relate and tune in to others, and put people at ease. They learn from others, and like learning in teams, comparing notes, socialising and teaching.

7   *Intrapersonal intelligence* – the intelligence of self-discovery. They prefer to work alone, like peace and quiet and often day-dream. They are intuitive, keep a diary, plan their time carefully and are independent. They learn by setting personal goals, taking control of their learning and reflecting on their experiences.

Gardner also added another intelligence, 'naturalistic', which is generally taken to mean the intelligence which allows individuals to relate to the natural world, to classify and to demonstrate a natural expertise in developing patterns, which can help the individual to develop order from chaos.

Once students understand their preferences and the more they understand about how they learn, they can use this knowledge to accelerate their learning and to make their learning experiences more meaningful.

Some creative students will be more 'whole-brained' and may well prefer to operate across a number of the intelligences. One of the most famous examples of this was Leonardo da Vinci. Without doubt Leonardo was exceptional; he embraced not only painting, drawing and sculpture but also civil engineering, architecture, inventing and other disciplines. From his journals we know that he applied the highest level of thought and attention to all of them.

Seven Da Vincian Principles

In *How to Think like Leonardo da Vinci* (1998), Michael Gelb describes 'Seven Da Vincian Principles' which will have a real resonance with creative people. He names the principles in Italian, and describes the Seven Da Vincian Principles as:

- *curiosita:* an insatiably curious approach to life and an unrelenting quest for continuous learning;
- *dimostrazione:* a commitment to test knowledge through experience, persistence, and a willingness to learn from mistakes;
- *sensazione:* the continual refinement of the senses, especially sight, as the means to enliven experience;
- *sfumato* (literally 'going up in smoke'): a willingness to embrace ambiguity, paradox and uncertainty;
- *arte/scienza:* the development of the balance between science and art, logic and imagination, or 'whole-brain' thinking;
- *corporalita:* the cultivation of grace, ambidexterity, fitness and poise;
- *connessione:* a recognition of and appreciation for the interconnectedness of all things and phenomena, or systems thinking.

He suggests that one, 'sfumato', is the most distinctive trait of highly creative people and that Leonardo probably possessed that trait more than anyone who has ever lived.

Gelb presents a host of ways of stimulating an individual's creativity. Consider his principle of 'curiosita'. Leonardo da Vinci carried a notebook with him at all times. Many creative people adopt such an approach. Richard Branson has been attributed with keeping a notebook. It is the only way that creative people are able to catch their ongoing creativity. Others keep them as a library of ideas and now, particularly in America, there is growth in illustrative journaling, which we discuss in more detail in Chapter 4. What many creative people find is that they often note down many ideas, which at the time burn passionately within them, and yet when they return to the books later they are surprised how many ideas they have forgotten. Leonardo's journals are said to be full of drawings, notes, personal finance records, paintings and plans for inventions. Gelb states that 18 sheets of Leonardo's notebooks were purchased by Bill Gates for 30.8 million dollars in 1994.

In Gelb and Gardner's work we see how people's preferences range across more than one intelligence, and yet many employment tests place a higher emphasis on verbal and mathematical reasoning.

Encouraging curiosity

Gelb also states that, as a child, Leonardo possessed intense curiosity about the world around him:

> Great minds go on asking confounding questions with the same intensity throughout their lives. Leonardo's childlike sense of wonder and insatiable curiosity, his breadth and depth of interest, and his willingness to question accepted knowledge never abated. Curiosita fuelled the wellspring of his genius throughout his adult life.

Many gifted children are similar. For some parents and teachers the incessant asking of 'Why?' from a young child can almost drive them to distraction, but it is from this base that the best learning takes place. Learning driven by a natural curiosity is absorbing and helps develop concentration. As stated in the Introduction, helping children make the connections is equally important. One of the real challenges for business organisations is encouraging their employees to gain an overview of the business and to be curious about what other parts are doing. Fostering that connectivity in young children and students promotes a valuable skill for later life, and connectivity is one of the competences that often identifies high-potential employees.

As well as working with Tony Buzan and the Mind Mapping® process, Gelb also makes reference to the work of Howard Gardner and his theory of multiple intelligences.

Emotional intelligence

Increasingly, individuals and organisations are recognising the richness that can be found through examining areas which are more personal, such as the Emotional Competence framework identified by Daniel Goleman in his book *Working with Emotional Intelligence* (1998).

Although it may seem that 'emotional intelligence' is a recent entrant into our vocabulary, it has in fact been acknowledged for a much longer period. Goleman suggests that a number of people have defined 'emotional intelligence', including Howard Gardner and Peter Salovey and John Mayer in the 1990s, who defined emotional intelligence 'in terms of being able to monitor and regulate one's own and others' feelings and to use feelings to guide thought and action'.

His own definition includes 'five basic emotional and social competencies:

- Self-awareness
- Self-regulation
- Motivation
- Empathy
- Social skills'

Goleman's work moves emotional intelligence into the arena of emotional competence by further defining 25 emotional competencies and explaining that individuals will have a profile of strengths and limits, but that:

> the ingredients for outstanding performance require only that we have strengths in a given number of these competencies, typically at least six or so, and that the strengths be spread across all five areas of emotional intelligence. In other words there are many paths to excellence.

What Goleman and others have done is to introduce the concept of another type of intelligence and the suggestion that students' skills with people are as important to the organisations that might recruit them as their IQ, qualifications and other experience and potential.

Many organisations are also recognising the impact of this in their retention and development of key workers. These personal competencies, together with other traits and characteristics, present vital clues to creating meaningful learning experiences for the students leaving schools, colleges and universities.

If the young person that you are working with enjoys the learning experience, they are more likely to learn and remember. If they are *told* they need to learn something, their willingness to learn will depend on the respect that they have for the person telling them and their desire to learn. If their desire to learn is driven by a personal curiosity and they learn in a way that reflects their preferred learning style, it is likely that their own enthusiasm and interest will make the learning more meaningful and memorable. In order to create meaningful learning experiences, teachers, lecturers, trainers and workplace coaches and individual learners could do so much more to develop effective learning patterns.

Ironically, much pre-school and early years learning does focus on more stimulating ways of learning. Unfortunately, many of the opportunities to really experience learning seem to disappear as individuals progress through school and career. One way that this can be developed is through the use of blended learning (see Chapter 8).

The hidden message from my school, I eventually realized, was not only crippling it was wrong. The world is not an unsolved puzzle, waiting for the occasional genius to unlock its secrets. The world, or most of it, is an empty space waiting to be filled. That realization changed my life. I did not have to wait and watch for the puzzles to be solved, I could jump into the space myself. I was free to try out my ideas, invent my own scenarios, create my own futures.

(Charles Handy, *Beyond Certainty*, 1995)

4 Unlocking the windows of the mind

How to create an inspiring learning environment

The young child who is totally open-minded, who adores drawing and painting and who colors all things all colors, who asks incessant questions, and who can imagine that the box in which his birthday present came is an infinite variety of things, including an airplane, a house, a cave, a tank, a boat, a spaceship gradually becomes trained to write notes in only one color, to ask very few questions (especially not 'stupid' ones – that is, the most interesting ones!), to keep the millions of lusting-for-action muscle fibers still for hours on end, and to become increasingly aware of his incompetences in art, singing, intelligence and physical sports. In time the child thus graduates into an adult who considers himself uncreative, and who has 'progressed' from being able to think of millions of uses for a box to being able to think of hardly any uses for anything.

(Tony Buzan, *Head Strong*, 2001)

Some people go through life with a very grey perspective; others live their lives through their senses, drawing inspiration from the richness of colour or sound around them. Some have a perspective of optimism; others start with their glass already half-empty.

The concept behind this chapter is to specifically focus on the learning experiences of young people, to identify what conditions need to be present for young people and their teachers to be most creative and, importantly, to try to release the potential that the young people could take with them from school to school and ultimately into their lives beyond formal education. This chapter has also been one of the hardest to write, as in reality there is no limit to the creative activities that you can undertake with children. As I write this line, another teacher will have had a fantastically creative idea which has only just been born. This chapter can only touch the surface of creative activities. If you took a helicopter with an X-ray camera and flew across the country looking into schools you would see an amazing array of colourful projects, themes, displays and children's imaginative work stimulated by very creative teachers. Sadly, what you might also see are some schools that are less hopeful, some individual classrooms that are lacking in inspiration, and some teachers or lecturers who wish that they were somewhere else.

My belief is that every individual is unique, but there are some people who are living with something else that presents them and the people or organisations with which they interact with the opportunity to really make a difference:

> Artists are people whose 'real' job, no matter what their paying job, is the pursuit of excellence by listening carefully and well to what is trying to be born through them. Artists are not fragile, but we are delicate. We are subject to the weather conditions in our life, just as a long gray winter spent indoors can cause depression, so, too, a period where our creative life is led without the sunshine of encouragement can cause a season of despair . . . We cannot control everything and everybody in our creative environment . . . For most of us the idea that we can listen to ourselves, trust ourselves and value ourselves is a radical leap of faith. The idea that we can tell ourselves 'Hey you are doing pretty well and so much better than you did last year' amounts to a revolution.
>
> (Julia Cameron, *Walking in this World*, 2002
> – see 'Recommended reading')

This extract from *Walking in this World* does not apply just to 'artists' in the purely artistic world. It also applies to the majority of human beings. We often have to work against negative feedback from others which tells how well we are not doing, rather than how well we are doing.

Why is creativity important?

'Creativity' is one of those words which prompts very different reactions from different people. For some their eyes glaze over as if you are about to enter one of those 'soft areas' where they feel very uncomfortable. For others it prompts strong debate: 'You can't teach creativity. People either have it or they don't.' Alternatively, those who have experienced the power of being in 'flow' talk powerfully about how special the experience is.

Pure creativity often has to fight through so much rubbish and junk, accumulated facts that were given to us through our education that we have never used. Day-to-day rubbish is sent to us through junk mail, emails, memos or even meetings that we are meant to attend, and yet through the window a vial of inspiration essence beckons if only we could reach out and pick it up.

It is hard to anchor down some of the key points that need to be explored, and much of this is because creativity is about feeling. Creative people, when inspired, have an energy. They often use their senses; they often operate through multiple intelligences. It can also be a tiring experience, when they may lock themselves away for hours working on an idea or a project.

Many working environments are far too serious and lacking in inspiration. People who naturally enjoy exploring their creativity do see life through a different optic.

They also may be driven by a force which gives them an energy that others cannot quite comprehend. They have a passion to make something work and to find a new way of doing things. They often want to 'make a real difference', not just within their own working environment but for the greater good of the organisation or humanity in general. In pursuit of this they can become completely absorbed, and very frustrated when others do not have the same passions. This can be particularly true when they are waiting for a response or feedback from others. Because they invest so much personal energy and time in an embryonic idea, it can be very hard for them to then have to wait while their idea goes through a bureaucratic process before they get a decision about the acceptance of the idea. This often prompts creative individuals to leave an organisation and to work for themselves.

We all have the capacity to be creative. However, what has happened to many people is that they have gradually turned off the tap of self-belief that they can be creative:

> Every day we slaughter our finest impulses. That is why we get a heartache when we read the lines written by a master and recognize them as our own, as the tender shoots, which we stifled because we lacked the faith to believe in our own powers, our own criterion of truth and beauty. Every man when he gets quiet, when he becomes desperately honest with himself, is capable of uttering profound truths.
>
> (Henry Miller)

> Creativity doesn't mean just making things up out of thin air. It means seeing and feeling the world so vividly that you can put together connections and patterns that help to explain reality. It means you see the beauty in the world rather than trying to hide from it. It's scary isn't it?
>
> (Danny Gregory, *The Creative License*, 2006)

What Gregory highlights is the fact that creativity is 'hard-wired into all of us', but gradually, through our day-to-day decisions, the career choices we make and the lifestyle we choose, many people move away from their natural creative impulses, to take what they believe are more responsible routes.

However, creativity is not important just to a selection of creative occupations; creative thinking is essential in almost every aspect of our lives, which is why it is vital to keep the spirit of creativity alive in our schools. One of the greatest leaders of creativity was Dr E. Paul Torrance, who died in 2003 aged 87. He became known around the world as the 'father of creativity'. He was a prolific writer, and in 2001 his book *Manifesto: A Guide to Developing a Creative Career* was published, including the results of a 40-year longitudinal study, the only one of its kind. After reviewing over 50 definitions of 'creative thinking', he defined it as follows: 'Creative thinking is the process of sensing difficulties, problems, gaps in information, missing elements, something askew, making guesses and hypotheses about the solution of these deficiencies; evaluating and testing these hypotheses; possibly revising them and finally communicating the result.' He invented the benchmark method for quantifying creativity. The Torrance Tests of Creative Thinking (TTCT) helped shatter the theory that IQ tests alone were sufficient to gauge real intelligence. The Torrance Tests took two forms, verbal and figural.

The verbal test consisted of students inventing uses for common things, such as stuffed animals, and were measured against the following criteria. First they were asked 'How would you make this a better toy?' Then students' responses were measured against:

- *fluency:* thinking of many ideas;
- *flexibility:* thinking of different ways to do or use things;
- *originality:* thinking of different unique things;
- *elaboration:* thinking of details and embellishments to an idea.

The figural tests required students to incorporate simple shapes like circles, or abstract line drawings, into more complete pictures. The results were judged on some of the same criteria as for the verbal tests, with the addition of other creativity indicators such as humour and emotionality.

In *Guiding Creative Talent* (1962) (see 'Recommended reading'), Paul Torrance gives all the details behind how the tests were created and administered.

He also referred to something called the 'inventivlevel', which was adapted from the US Patent Office. It contained the following criteria:

- *Stride forward.* Does this idea present a new and original plan? How useful is this idea? Does this usefulness extend in a practical, realistic direction?
- *Newness.* Is this idea unusual or remarkable? Is it of recent origin? Does it show innovation or new effects?
- *Challenging and thought provoking.* Does the idea lead to new and additional ideas? Does it, or can it, generate new ideas?
- *Rarity.* Is the idea different from those generally given? Is it produced by only a few individuals?
- *Constructiveness.* Does the idea tell how to bring about the change, apply the principle or solve the problem?

- *Surprise.* Does the idea produce astonishment, wonder or surprise?

Torrance's tests are still in use today. More information is available from www.coe.uga.edu/torrance/.

Another model that you will see used in many contexts to describe the act of creativity is the one suggested by Joseph Wallas in 1926:

- *Preparation.* This is the primarily factual stage of researching and data gathering. You may have an idea of an area worth exploring, but it is unconfirmed. It may be nothing more than a 'hunch' or feeling.
- *Incubation.* The ideas are beginning to form, but you let them simmer. You leave them at the back of your mind while you are doing other things. You bring them forward from time to time but are not ready to act on them.
- *Illumination.* This is the reason why a light bulb is often used to symbolise idea generation or creativity. It is that stage or moment when you realise that you know what it all means or why you have spent so long thinking about something. It is often described as the 'aha' moment.
- *Verification.* This is the checking-out period, when you talk to others, share the idea, refine it, qualify it and make sure that it really is worth investing time and resources in to take it forward to the next stage.

Other writers, including Goleman, have made reference to the work of Jules Henri Poincaré and others in developing this model to include other stages, notably:

- *Execution.* This is another important stage, and it may sound the death knell for many ideas, as it takes a different set of behaviours and often requires the inventor to communicate and collaborate with others.

How can this be applied in the classroom?

Apart from actually using the tests with students, we can also apply the principles in day-to-day teaching.

If we examine the four areas identified by Torrance, there are a number of activities that we can create to encourage children to develop creativity:

- *Fluency:* thinking of many ideas. This is about generating ideas. In the context of the Torrance Test about making the toy a better toy, you are trying to encourage a flow of ideas. If the toy is only stuffed, ask the children how it could be improved or what would make it a better toy – fitting a sound box or wheels, attaching a lead, with today's technology allowing a parent to record a message and put it inside, and so on. This can be applied to any item. Try to choose something that is appropriate for your class and age group.

- *Flexibility:* thinking of different ways to do or use things. This is a popular creative thinking technique used in many creative thinking contexts with adults as well as children. Show the class an item and ask them how many different uses they can think of for the item. There are ways that you can encourage this line of thought. Once they have exhausted the common uses, you can make additional suggestions:

  What could be added to this item to create a different use?
  What if we changed the colour?
  What if it changed shape?
  What if we put it with something else?
  What if we made it move?
  What if we could use more senses with it?

- *Originality:* thinking of different unique things. In this context you are trying to get the children to really think 'outside the box'. In his test, Torrance suggested the following instructions: 'Think of the cleverest, most interesting, and most unusual use you can for this toy dog (monkey), other than as a plaything. For example it could be used as a pin cushion as it is. If you could make it larger and stronger you could use it to sit on.'

- *Elaboration.* Show the children an everyday item, or a picture of the item, and ask them to think of additional things that the item could do over and above what it can do currently. For example, we know that a vacuum cleaner cleans. What else could it be used for? Depending on the age of the children you could then talk about the work of James Dyson and how he took an ordinary everyday item and found a revolutionary way of changing it. You could also apply the 'inventivlevel' criteria mentioned above to the idea. This could then be developed into the work of other inventors, what innovation means, the challenges faced, and encouraging the children to come up with their own inventions.

Tony Buzan however, in *Head Strong* (2001), using a similar technique suggests that the mind can go even further. Defining creative ideas, he suggests that they are 'original, removed from the norm and as such they are usually exciting'. To put this into practice, he states:

> Give yourself exactly two minutes to write down, as fast as you can, every single use you can think of for a coat hanger . . . Your goal is then to add up your total and divide by two to give your average output per minute.

He then states that:

> The average number of uses for a coat hanger per minute score ranges from 0 (and this is with some effort!) through to 4–5 (which is the global average) to 8 (which is good brain-stormer level) to 12 (which is exceptional and rare) to 16 (which is Thomas Edison-genius level). If people are given as long as they want to think up as many uses as they can for a coat hanger the average score is 20–30 uses.

He also states that this test is considered 'statistically reliable': 'if you take the test on any given day, then take it again years later, it is believed that your results will be similar'. However, he suggests that the rigidly taught mind will assume that 'uses' are standard ones. He suggests that:

> the Mentally Literate® and more flexibly taught brain will see far more opportunities for creative interpretations of the question, and therefore will generate both more ideas and of a higher quality

... The creative genius will therefore break all the ordinary boundaries, and will include in the list of uses many 'far out' (away from the norm!) applications, such as 'melting a five-ton metal coat-hanger and pouring it into a giant mold to make the hull of a boat'.

For more information, visit www.mind-mapping.co.uk/.

Tools and techniques

Before you can inspire others you need to inspire yourself.

Despite all the demands of the curriculum, there is still a need to try creating time for yourself. Little by little, as if chipping away at a rock, there is coming a realisation by teaching organisations that teachers need time to develop their own skills and professionalism. Creativity is no different from any other discipline. It is not something that is 'nice to do'. It takes time to develop an individual's creativity. If you expose yourself to richness of experience you can stimulate your creativity.

However well motivated you are, there may be times when you need to recharge or to be inspired to enable you to work more effectively with others. When you find that your creativity is being stifled, take a break and do something completely different. Take regular time out to indulge you. Use others for support and for bouncing ideas off, however crazy. Build on initial fleeting thoughts to anchor more tangible concepts. Unlearn lessons from childhood. Say 'I can' instead of 'I can't'. Tune into your surroundings by being inspired by a view, music and space.

Some people find that they need to create a special environment to be creative. This may be a special place, a desk or a room at home which becomes the focus for your thinking time. Even just carrying a picture with you can create hope in what might be a tough teaching day. Other people go running or take part in some other kind of physical activity.

Many people feel that their best ideas occur when they are least expecting it or doing something else. However, once they start to flow you want to try to capture them. It is also important to record everything, as even the most insignificant points may ultimately become an important feature of the end result. Equally, if you find that the ideas are not flowing it is important not to force the process; it is better to leave it and do something else. Often people find that by doing something completely different their mind will suddenly start generating ideas. Creative thinking also takes place at night through something called the Theta process, which is when the mind produces its own solutions, which are there when you awake.

One of the toughest parts of being driven by your creative thoughts is controlling it and channelling it into a normal working environment. The outpourings of ideas, which are full of richness, cannot necessarily be managed within the confines of a normal working day. As a result, where an individual is expected to work within the constraints of a time-frame, frustration and tiredness and ultimately lack of motivation often occur. What do you do when you find that your mind is racing at 2 a.m., particularly if it is focusing on a non-work-related subject that is close to your heart and you know that the next morning you are expected to teach a difficult class or attend a meeting, which will sap all the remaining energy that you have? All you want to do is to stay with the idea that demands your attention. This is a challenge faced by all creative people. There is also the need to respect and acknowledge the needs of others. What is interesting is that if you have the inner flow of energy or ideas you need very little to stimulate it.

Mihalyi Csikzentmihalyi, a University of Chicago psychologist, described this feeling as 'flow' (1990). He says that we experience 'flow' when we feel in control of our actions and are masters of our own fate. What he discovered was that when people were experiencing 'flow' their state was very similar: there was a sensation of pleasure, they felt as if they were floating, they were totally immersed in what they were doing, they forgot their worries and they lost a sense of time. One of the challenges is to focus, because so many thoughts come floating into your mind it sometimes seems impossible to capture all the richness before the ideas dry up or, as is more likely, we are interrupted.

Pure creative thinking is often fast; the speed of creative thought is frightening in terms of speed and complexity, because when your mind is flowing it is almost the equivalent of a mental meltdown. On a particularly good day the senses collide – hearing, seeing, feeling, sensing. However, capturing this so that you can share the information with others is also important. Techniques like Mind Mapping® help in allowing the thoughts to be captured on one page, with the interconnections.

As suggested in Chapter 3, you may find tools and techniques like Buzan's Mind Mapping®, de Bono's Six Thinking Hats or brainstorming help you to focus, but if you have the ability to be creative all you really need is a means of recording, because when you find yourself in a creative state it is a force that cannot really be controlled: it has an energy and speed all of its own. Equally, it can disappear at will too. The good news is that it will return, often when you least expect it, nudging at the corners of your mind, saying 'Remember me?'

When working within the classroom, there are specific ways in which you can develop the broadest approach not just to developing creativity, but to the growth of all effective learning. When you are creating learning experiences for others, take time to help them explore their own creativity. Use a variety of sources to help them recognise the rich variety and ways of doing things differently.

Positive thinking

There are now probably enough self-help books to be well on the way to encircling the world if we laid them end to end. Many are based on the theories of neurolinguistic programming (NLP). Over the years NLP has gained respect in many organisations in the areas of personal development and communication. NLP practitioners describe it as an art and a science of personal excellence. It is based on a set of models, skills and techniques for thinking and acting effectively. It was started in the 1970s by John Grinder and Richard Bandler. From their initial work, NLP developed into two complementary directions, first as a process for discovering patterns of excellence in any field and second as the effective way of thinking and communicating used by outstanding people.

The 'neuro' part of NLP refers to the neurological processes of seeing, hearing, feeling, tasting and smelling, i.e. our senses. The 'linguistic' part refers to the importance of language in both our thought processes and our communication. For example:

- *Visual.* You think in pictures and you represent ideas, memory and imagination as mental images.
- *Auditory.* You think in sounds. These sounds could be voices, or noises of common everyday sounds.
- *Feelings.* You represent thoughts as feelings that might be internal emotion or the thought of physical touch. Taste and smell are often included in this category.

People often find that they have a preference in the way that they think and communicate.

'Programming' refers to the way we can programme our own thoughts and behaviour, in much the same way that a computer is programmed to do specific things. There is not space within this book to explore NLP fully, but there is a range of books available on the subject and courses available. See Chapter 12 for more details.

In the context of positive thinking, there is one technique that is almost immediately applicable, which is to do with a shift in mindset. Many adults and young people have a negative view of themselves, and over time the negative programming becomes fixed. We discuss this more in Chapter 7. However, by the use of positive thinking the brain can shift from 'I can't' to 'I can'. It has to be a realistic shift, and it is a valuable tool to give to any student. It is the basis of all good sports coaching. It is about focusing on what is achievable and realistic.

The first action can be to encourage individuals to identify what they do currently that they are proud of, for example 'I am good at art', and next to identify what they want to achieve, for example 'I am working towards being a graphic designer'. The important action is not to set people up to fail. In the area of personal development, it's about identifying what they want to achieve in their life and helping them work towards it. It is really important that they realise that very little success is achieved overnight – people who are successful have to work at it – but equally encourage them to recognise the baby steps that they take towards achieving their goal. In this context the visualisation exercise below can really help them to build a picture of what it could be like if they achieved their dream.

Visualisation

Using techniques such as visualisation and storytelling, the skilled teacher can transport learners out of the most uninspiring environments to unlock their imaginations and creativity. It is also about the teacher's own sources of creativity and inspiration.

Visualisation is a very powerful tool in helping individuals to see alternatives. However, initially some individuals will need a lot of support to realise its potential. Remember the saying 'If you keep on doing what you always did, you always get what you always got.' Creativity is about enabling people to see alternatives so that they don't always get what they always got. Achieving this shift in perspective will take time. Helping the individual to take small incremental steps towards another vision should ultimately lead to them beginning to have another view of the world.

One way of using visualisation is to create a mood board. This can be used for almost any activity, but is most effective when it is about something meaningful for the student. A mood board is a made up of pictures and images to create a 'mood'. It is a technique often used by advertising agencies to create an impression in the minds of its customers, which will help them to identify with a particular product or service. Using old magazines, glue, scissors and a large piece of paper, students create the mood board. For example, if a student created a mood board to illustrate the ambition of going travelling around the world it could have lots of pictures of exotic places like the Taj Mahal, San Francisco Bridge, the New York skyline, Sydney Opera House, the Eiffel Tower and the Pyramids. There could be sunsets and sunrises, waterfalls, tropical plants, palm trees, koala bears, tigers, Italian pasta, Indian curries and Moroccan bazaars; brightly coloured silks and jewels – ruby, emerald, topaz and turquoise; glistening white beaches, sea, sea and more sea; endless blue skies, aeroplanes, helicopters, the Orient Express, ski-jets, scuba divers, dolphins, people smiling and hands shaking. The student could add words like 'East', 'West', 'Golden Gate', 'sunshine', 'exotic', 'paradise', 'happiness', 'freedom' and 'space'.

The secret is encourage your students' minds to wander and to encourage them just to go through the magazines selecting the words and images that appeal. Ask the students just to cut out the images, but do not attempt to put them in any order at first. Let the students take their time; let their thoughts take their own path. When they have gathered enough, let them start laying them on the card. Encourage them not to stick them down until they feel that they have started to create a 'mood' and they are happy with the positioning. As well as being used for positive activities like the mood board about travelling, this technique can be used to deal with more difficult circumstances and, in this case, may need sensitive support when the student or child reveals issues that are personal and important to them. Chapter 7 examines self-esteem. A mood board technique can be used to help a child or student create an image of who they would like to be and then with careful support a teacher could work with the individual to achieve some of these ambitions.

When you feel the students have finished, ask them to sit back and review what the overall picture is saying to them. When I have used this exercise as part of a workshop, there is so much dis-cussion about the words and images that have been chosen. Often by working in this way the senses take over, allowing students the freedom to portray hopes and dreams that may surprise them. Depending on the group and the topic you may encourage them to share their mood boards with a partner.

Storyboarding

Another technique is to encourage children to imagine that they are going to make a short documentary. Ask them to create storyboards of how the action would take place, what scenes would be required, who would be interviewed, what locations would be needed, what the commentary would say and what the key messages would be. Many schools now have access to equipment, either their own or equipment made available through links with colleges or local businesses, which would allow this activity to be carried through to the actual filming. A similar process can be used with digital photography, and from both avenues the film can be shown or an exhibition mounted.

Illustrative journaling

This is a technique that has grown rapidly in popularity, particularly in the US. It's a little like graffiti in a book, where people use journals to write, draw, paint and collect items from their daily lives. The principle is very similar to the notepads of Leonardo da Vinci, but many end up almost as works of art.

Another linked concept is altered books, which is defined as taking any book and altering it to create a new work of art. As with making collages, the advantage of all of these techniques is that they allow freedom of expression, can be very personal to the individual and can be readily used to express creativity without high levels of technical artistic ability. One of the main reasons why people shy away from expressing themselves in paint or drawing is that early on in life they convince themselves that they lack the technical ability. This is one way of dispelling that fear.

Storytelling

As well as professional storytellers who may visit schools, there is a wealth of opportunities to use storytelling in the classroom. From the reception end-of-day story, through to local people coming in and telling their part of local history, to children reading out their own stories, there are many opportunities to both create and read stories. This is helped by the upswing in interest in reading brought about by books such as the *Lord of the Rings* or the 'Harry Potter' and 'Narnia' series. Help children to explore their writing through how they organise it, how original it is, how rich in detail and how meaningful it is. Use every opportunity to demystify writing. Encourage children to write something each day.

Music

One of the multiple intelligences is musical intelligence. As we discussed in Chapter 3, this is the intelligence of rhythm, music and lyrics. People with this may play musical instruments, often sing or hum to themselves, and like relaxing to music. They learn by using music and may use rhymes to help them remember things. It is also part of NLP that some people think in sounds. These sounds could be voices, or noises of common everyday sounds, yet some classes are devoid of any auditory stimulation, apart from the voice of the teacher. Some activities lend themselves very well to having appropriate background music – not all the time, but a carefully selected range of music that can both calm students down and uplift them. Most classical collections have a blend that can work well in a classroom, but vary it; think about world music; think about some music used in advertising; run a classroom session about the use of music in advertising, play music and ask the class to identify which advert it is linked to. This can be extended to a quiz where you show students a very small part of a well-known brand logo and see if they can identify it. Talk about some of the key messages behind branding, and what emotions some of the big brands are trying to create in our minds.

Creative problem solving

Creative thinking is not just about the creative arts; it applies right across the curriculum, helping students to identify alternatives and offering support as they work through options. Often the issue or problem simply seems too big a challenge. Helping them to identify the issue and break it down into manageable chunks is an important first step; then they can move forward using steps like these below:

- Identify the problem.
- Think around it.
- Seek the involvement and views of interested people with differing views.
- Isolate the problem and pay attention to it.
- Use a variety of problem-solving techniques.
- Think around the problem and explore all ideas and options.
- Focus on solutions in a structured way.
- Agree an action plan for implementation.
- Review and evaluate the outcomes.

Again, working in teams can broaden the perspectives and create different solutions.

Brainstorming

This is one of the simplest yet most effective techniques for working with groups. Using a blank piece of paper, blackboard or whiteboard, you note as many thoughts as possible randomly, without any attempt to rank or order them. This technique is designed to help with the flow of ideas, and there are important rules: no editing, no qualifying and no restricting. The concept works because one person's thoughts often stimulate others, and by not interrupting each other the ideas flow very quickly. The activity often also creates an energy and an element of fun within a group.

SWOT

This is a commonly used business technique, but it has real value in schools and colleges, as it encourages young people to take a more objective view of ideas. By dividing a page or board in four and adding four headings the group may analyse their idea. Strengths and weaknesses are perceived as current and internal issues, and opportunities and threats are seen as external.

Creative use of themes

Coombes School (see page 61) makes great use of cycles and themes, and this is a great way to encourage a holistic view of learning. Traditionally, infant schools have developed very imaginative and creative learning experiences around themes, e.g. water, fire or transport, but the concept of cross-functional creativity tends to die out as the child progresses through the different levels of schooling and, by secondary level, many schools focus more on single subjects rather than develop cross-subject thinking. It is an issue that is also demonstrated in many businesses, where different functions become silos of talent; therefore encouraging 'joined-up' thinking is a very valuable skill for young people to develop.

Creating an abundance of good ideas

All the above are just a very small taster of a whole range of techniques that can be used to stimulate creative thinking. However, as every good teacher knows, every day can create a new idea or a new way of teaching something. Teachers have a reputation of being a little like magpies: they see something glinting and swoop to pick it up and take it back to their classroom. They take the original idea, embellish it, change it and interpret it in different ways. This is how great learning evolves and how it needs to continue to grow. It's also about sharing ideas and best practice. Chapter 12 gives more examples of ideas, sources of information and websites which underpin the growth of creativity.

So what else can teachers do to stimulate children's creativity?

Despite the demands of the curriculum, teachers at all stages of a child's development can recognise some fundamentals which are more likely to encourage than inhibit creativity.

Help them develop self-belief

Shad Helmstetter, in *What to Say when You Talk to Yourself* (1998) (see 'Recommended reading'), gave a very graphic example of his desire to play a musical instrument and to be a member of the school band. He tried out with a number of other students, playing on an instrument that was totally alien to him. Later in the day he overheard the band director telling his class teacher that not only could he not play in the band but he had no musical ability and would never be able to play a musical instrument!

It was years later before he finally got up enough courage to rent a piano and learn some notes. It took him 20 years to find out the band director was wrong! He contrasted that with a young child who overheard an old man tell his mother 'that young Michael would be very creative, and he would grow up to be creative'. That child grew up to become the dean of Walt Disney University. Both examples illustrate the power of influence that we can have on young people and their self-esteem.

It is well researched that many creative people actually had to overcome enormous challenges in their schooling. Business people, famous sports people, artists and many others had to overcome negative feedback from teachers or parents. Others have had to overcome personal adversity such as the loss of a parent or other early-life traumas. In *Essential Motivation in the Classroom* (2002) (see 'Recommended reading'), Ian Gilbert describes some key strategies for motivating children and young people. He describes how Japanese culture has a form of internal motivation called 'mastery'. This is the process of 'trying to be better than no one other than yourself'. He also quotes John Wooden in *Practical Modern Basketball*:

> True success can be attained only through self-satisfaction, in knowing you did everything within the limits of your ability to become the very best you are capable of being . . . Therefore, in the final analysis, only the individual himself can correctly determine his success.

Feed their imagination

Encourage them to dream, to explore fantasies and to write imaginatively. Help them to develop tools for creative writing. Invite writers, artists and storytellers in. Read to them and encourage them to use their senses, not just for sensory perception in primary schools, but maintaining the process as they go through secondary school. Encourage them to read the best, to develop the skills of literary criticism and to be able to give constructive feedback. Help them to explore their writing through how they organise it, how original it is, how rich in detail and how meaningful it is. Equally, allowing people to share ideas is an important part of the creative process. Companies like Disney use a technique called 'displayed thinking', where ideas are incubated by a continuous process of brainstorming when the originators of the ideas allow others to add their input. This could work very well in schools to encourage the sharing of ideas.

Help them express themselves

Creativity can be expressed in so many ways. It is a mistake to see it only in the context of the obvious artistic interpretation, as creativity has a relevance in every single discipline. Idea generation is an underpinning skill needed in every school. Think about the dictionary definition, 'Inventive and imaginative, creating, or able to create'. Every discovery or advance in science, engineering, geography, history or any other subject or innovation is based on someone's ability to see things differently. Great inventors, discoverers and scientists have been ridiculed as much as great musicians, writers or artists.

It is also important, as already mentioned, to build self-belief. Being creative takes great personal courage and the willingness to go where others have failed before. Expressing your embryonic views to others or taking risk needs to be built on sure foundations:

> People who lack a flair for innovation . . . typically miss the larger picture and get enmeshed in details, and so deal with problems only slowly, even tediously. The fear of risk makes them shy away from novel ideas. And when they try to find solutions they often fail to realize that what worked in the past is not always the answer for the future . . . People who are uncomfortable with risk become critics and naysayers. Defensive and cautious, they may constantly deride, or undermine innovative ideas.
>
> (Daniel Goleman, *Working with Emotional Intelligence*, 1998)

Give them time

However focused on the curriculum we are, we should also spend creative time with children, listening to them and answering their questions. Encourage them to be curious, do things together, believe in their ambitions, and instil in them a 'can do' attitude. Be interested in them; help them to feel good about themselves.

Give them positive feedback. We already know that many people have their motivation squeezed out of them by negative feedback. So many really talented young people's development is capped by other people. We are all culpable; we're all busy; so often you hear children ignored or shut out of conversations because the adults are focused on other things or, worse still, because we just don't listen.

Allow their voice to be heard

Creative children in particular are curious; they ask questions at the most awkward time; they also ask the most awkward questions. They may challenge our view or they may turn the tables on an unprepared teacher, showing a depth of knowledge beyond their years. They ask the 'What if?' questions to which we may not have the answer. Encouraging them to go and find the answer or allowing them to explore, to take their knowledge further and to share it with others with encouragement as part of an exploring classroom is a valuable support to the creative child.

Protect their environment

A few years ago I went to a UK university to talk about innovation and creativity. As I arrived I was faced with a concrete grey building. I walked along soulless corridors until I reached the office of the lecturer whom I was due to meet. As space for meetings was at a premium, I was taken into one of the lecture rooms for our meeting. The ceiling was low, there was little natural light and the walls were completely bare. I imagined what it must have been like to be a student in that environment, totally relying on the imagination and stimulation of the lecturer.

I contrasted it with a course I had attended at the Disney Institute in Orlando, where the whole campus exuded creativity and passion for learning. Not only were the staff enthusiastic, but also you were given privileged access to animators and behind-the-scenes visits, and were actively encouraged to jump in with both feet to explore your creativity. Both examples are at opposite ends of the learning experience, but it should be possible to bring some kind of magic into every learning experience.

One very real issue for many students is the need either to leave work in lockers or to carry it on their backs. This means that many young people have no sense of their own space. In the world of work this is similar to hot-desking, and research has shown that for some adults this has created some dissatisfaction, as actually having the opportunity to personalise their own space is quite important. Therefore trying to create environments which are stimulating for students as well as children is important.

Focus on developing their multiple intelligences

Teachers looking to stimulate children only have to look at the underpinning thoughts behind multiple intelligences to identify a whole year's lesson plans and more, but there is also the principle of recognising that we all learn differently.

Most nursery and primary schools are recognised for the wealth of visual stimulation that they give their students. However, as children move from nursery, to infant, to junior and finally to secondary and tertiary education, the level of visual stimulation seems to drop incrementally. If we think about Gardner's 'multiple intelligences' and Gelb's Seven Da Vincian Principles, it appears that many of our secondary and tertiary environments are lacking in the basic stimuli that create the best learning experiences. If we add in a teacher or lecturer who just 'tells', it is no wonder that the minds of our most creative children wander. There is a lot of discussion about using blended learning solutions, but this will work only if an integrated approach is adopted and the best use of technology is applied together with a focus on learning. (This is discussed in more detail in Chapter 8.) An excellent example of multiple intelligences in action is Writhlington School Orchid Project (see Chapter 9).

Connect with the creative community

One of the very real challenges about creativity is connecting with the local creative community. The nature of many creative activities is such that many creative people are self-employed and work in isolation, and so connecting with them may be difficult. But it is worth exploring what exists locally; one place to start is with Creative Partnerships. Based at Arts Council England, Creative Partnerships has a unique approach to working with schools. It first helps schools to identify their individual needs and then enables them to develop long-term, sustainable partnerships with organisations and individuals, including architects, theatre companies, museums, cinemas, historic buildings, dance studios, recording studios, orchestras, film-makers, website designers and many others.

Other sources are through networking and watching the local press. For example, increasingly there are local schemes such as Made

in Cornwall, which links together a number of providers who produce products made in Cornwall. In Dorset, they run art weeks
where local artists open up their studios to the public. Every local
area is likely to have a source of information; one place to start is
your local council offices, or key in 'artists in . . .' into a search engine
and it is likely that you will find local contacts. Parents too will have
a range of talents. Connect with them and identify a directory of
parents' talent – and not just parents, but grandparents, aunts, uncles
and friends of the family as well. If you invite involvement, as you will
see in the Coombes School example that follows, there is no limit to
the contacts that you can make.

Creativity in practice

One very inspiring book is *The Creative School* by Bob Jeffrey and
Peter Woods (2003) (see 'Recommended reading'). It charts the
progress of one school, Coombes County Nursery and Infant
School, and how it successfully combined the National Curriculum
with a set of personal beliefs and values. The authors had been connected with the school since 1990. Between 1999 and 2001 they
conducted a sustained ethnographic project aimed at understanding
teaching and learning at the school in greater depth.

If you look at the school's website, you will find their mission
statement is 'With children at heart and mind' and their intention is
'To be a learning community of children and adults working in a
holistic way, by integrating spiritual, moral, aesthetic, physical, social,
emotional and intellectual strands into everyday practice'. The
photographs give a small taste of the types of activities that take place.
Jeffrey and Woods describe the ethos at the school as 'dynamism,
appreciation, captivation and care'. 'The school understands young
children as active agents who experiment with their bodies, emotions
and intellects . . . Teachers acknowledge the enormous capacity of
young children to take in an extensive variety of experiences in any
one day.'

In the ongoing pursuit of connectivity between school and
industry, this is a very similar description to Daniel Goleman's in
Working with Emotional Intelligence (1998). As Goleman describes:

The premium on emotional intelligence can only rise as organizations become increasingly dependent on the talents and creativity of workers who are independent agents … Such free agents suggest a future for work somewhat akin to the functioning of the immune system, where roaming cells spot a pressing need, spontaneously collect into a tightly knit, highly co-ordinated working group to meet that need and dissipate into a free agency as the job finishes. In an organizational context such groups may arise within and across organizational boundaries as demands require, then cease to exist once their task is accomplished … Such virtual teams can be especially agile because they are headed by whoever has the requisite skills rather than someone who happens to have the title 'manager'.

The children who are being educated at Coombes are experiencing learning in a way that potentially will lead them to develop into adults who are able to work in virtual teams or cross-functionally and dynamically contribute to the growth of an organisation or their own business. Critically, this approach needs to be continued as the children progress through secondary, further and higher education:

> Every week people visit the school to talk about their lives, perform their skills and reproduce their crafts: Irish dancers, Scottish bagpipe performers, harpists, artists, stonemasons, a military band … a specialist in children's songs and rhymes from America, a Muslim woman talking about her faith and culture. There are also environmental maintenance events such as sheep shearing, hedge building and willow-arch weaving. These talks, demonstrations or performances engage the children's interest and take them on something akin to a 'Grand Tour' of the world outside the school.

Sue Humphries, the head teacher at the time of the study, said:

> It's a sense of being engaged and intrigued by work that goes on around them. It's coming in to them from the community, via a national world and via a National Curriculum. It is by encouraging other nationals, by encouraging people with a

mark for talent, whether it's sewing, knitting or writing poetry. They are being connected to much wider artistic, work and spiritual concerns. In this way they are learning more than the National Curriculum, which I hope we are doing well, but these others are equally important, as is nursing the side of the child that is going to be empathetic, imaginative and tolerant.

Their whole approach to teaching is creative and dynamic. Thus the children 'refine their handwriting skills by practising on table-tops with shaving foam, chocolate mousse or talcum powder' and 'learn about sentence structure, full stops, capital letters, commas, question marks and speech marks by becoming human sentences. It is through playing with these writing conventions that children begin to understand them.' Humphries states that the approach encourages a 'slight element of risk and we perceive this to be essential if the creative approach to teaching and learning is to be maintained and taken forward'.

They use drama a lot, particularly in the history, RE and English curriculum. Jeffrey and Woods suggest that special mention should be made of science, which is the school's forte. Sue Humphries and her deputy, Susan Rowe, have written two books on science teaching at Key Stage 1 of the National Curriculum. The authors:

> aim to encourage the children to be active participants in experiences that are exciting, interesting and informative. We learn best what we enjoy doing. The books encourage the children to do, to discover and to evaluate to be true scientists.

So how do the SATs results compare at Coombes? Jeffrey and Woods state that, for the years 1997–2001, they are broadly in line with the national average in literacy and above average for maths. Teacher-assessed science shows above-average levels achieved. Results for 2001 also show an improvement in literacy and science over 2000, with maths about the same as in the previous year. However, maths was at a high point in 2000 with 94 per cent of Year 2 children reaching Level 2, which is the average target level for this age group. Jeffrey and Woods reported the head teacher at the time, Sue Humphries, as saying:

I don't think you can raise the standards every year. You have to look beyond this to the children reaching 18 years, a lifelong attitude. It is what is in their hearts; that is what makes us different. It gives us an ability to understand other people . . . The children are being connected to wider artistic concerns, work concerns and spiritual concerns. They are learning other things as well as the National Curriculum. We are nursing the side of the child that is going to be empathetic, imaginative and tolerant.

As part of my research for this book I contacted the current head teacher, Susan Rowe, and asked the question, 'Have you managed to continue meeting the external challenges of the National Curriculum without compromising your principles of child-centred education?' I received the following very prompt response, as well as an invitation to visit the school. 'Yes, we have! The children still come first in our book and the curriculum is designed to serve them, rather than the other way around!'

It is very easy to fixate on one excellent example of a good school, and I am sure that this school is by no means unique. Every day in many schools, committed teachers are providing dynamic learning experiences for children. What this example does illustrate is how, despite external influences, the school, through consistency of approach, has stayed true to its values and its determination to create a very special learning experience for its children. The example also highlights some of the key points that I raised in the Introduction. The school is playing a vital role in connecting the children not just to its parents, but to its feeder school, the local community and beyond to the wider world.

5 Coaching conversations

Often in a classroom it's not what you say, but how you say it. Traditionally, the more formal aspects of the curriculum were taught in one way and coaching was reserved for extra-curricular activities. This chapter will focus on how to create conversations which really engage the learner, how to encourage commitment and how to help your students create goals that are meaningful for them. Many good teachers are intuitively natural coaches, but not everyone works in this way.

Introducing a coaching environment can have a very far-reaching impact; teachers need to think about their very best learning experiences, to remember what inspired them and to think about how they can recreate special learning experiences. Inspiring teachers who perform the role of coach have a major contribution to make, and schools may need to recognise that in the future classroom teaching may need to become much more focused on the individual, and as a result small discussion groups or one-to-one coaching may occur more frequently than formal classroom sessions.

The more collaborative and forward-thinking schools recognise that young people do not need to be 'told' in the traditional sense. What young people do need is guidance, coaching and the sharing of wisdom. Developing these coaching skills takes time and needs to be demonstrated through models of best practice which are cascaded throughout the organisation. The implication of all this for organisations and teachers is a fundamental shift from teaching to learning. There is a distinct difference in ownership. Young people needs to own and take responsibility for their own learning, and there is huge importance in helping individuals realise their potential.

Everyone is different

Each individual learner who is taught is different, and every teacher will have a different teaching style. Recognising these differences is an important part of coaching and helping others to learn. What is fascinating is recognising how subtle these differences are. No two people will have exactly the same combination, and in this context we should never make broad assumptions about different learners.

One way that you can help individuals gain personal insight is by encouraging them to build an understanding of themselves. We cover this in more detail in Chapter 9, but it has a relevance here. Daniel Goleman, in *Working with Emotional Intelligence*, quotes a study carried out by Carnegie-Mellon University with several hundred 'knowledge workers':

> Superior performers intentionally seek out feedback, they *want* to hear how others perceive them, realising that this is valuable information. That may also be part of the reason people who are self-aware are better performers. Presumably their self-awareness helps them in a process of continuous improvement.

Knowing their strengths and weaknesses, and approaching their work accordingly, was a competence found in virtually every star performer. The authors of the study stated, 'Stars know themselves well.'

What is coaching?

There are many definitions of coaching, but in summary it creates some of the following:

- unlocking natural ability;
- treating each individual as a person;
- inspiring others to take action;
- giving really valuable feedback;

- making learning different and fun;
- encouraging personal ownership;
- increasing confidence and self-esteem;
- ways of celebrating success.

Coaching techniques

While much of coaching is natural and intuitive, there are a number of specific skills and techniques that are deployed in effective coaching.

Listening

How well do you listen? Do you really suspend your prejudices and listen to others with your whole mind? Often people are thinking about what they are going to say next, making assumptions about the individual or, worse still, thinking about something completely different. In a busy classroom this can be one of the hardest things to do. It is necessary to give people time to make their point, really listen to their responses and encourage others to do the same. Often the restrictions of the timetable mean that teachers have to keep the process moving; however, it is also possible to demonstrate that you really have listened to someone, by showing your understanding in your response to them or by following up with them one to one, where it is easier to focus on individual needs. It is also a valuable skill for everyone to gain. Setting exercises where young people have to interview each other and summarise their findings is one way of encouraging them to listen. In today's noise-driven society, encouraging children to manage silence is a valuable skill. Equally, helping them to recognise non-verbal behaviours, such as body language, posture, expressions and the messages in mime, is a useful learning experience for the world beyond school.

Questioning

Just as it is important to listen, it is equally important to question effectively. The ability to ask the right question at the right time is a fundamental part of effective teaching. Normally there is a pattern to effective questioning, but as well as acknowledging this pattern it is also important that the conversation is as natural as possible. Most conversations are built around a structure of questions, initially asking questions that a learner can respond to. These are classed as closed questions, and will normally gain yes or no answers. Once the class has settled, teachers can then move on to more open questions. These are normally structured around 'how', 'when', 'why', 'what' or 'where'. As the lesson develops, teachers can ask more probing or clarifying questions, such as 'Tell me more about . . .' or 'What exactly do you mean by that?' Importantly, questioning needs to be sensitive to individuals. Whenever you ask questions, do not confuse the student by asking multiple questions. Initially some may hesitate in their answer. Try to wait for a response. However, if someone really does not know the answer, move on and encourage others to answer. Don't keep putting the same individual under pressure to answer.

Giving feedback

As well as questioning and listening, there will be occasions when the student will receive feedback, and for the learner it will be absolutely critical to get it right. So often the feedback that individual students receive is not given in a sensitive and skilled manner. Here are some key steps that can be taken:

- Prepare carefully, think around the situation and think about how the learners might respond.
- Try to ensure that you have time to give meaningful feedback one to one rather than in front of their peers.
- Always ask for their views first. It will give you a starting point.
- Always start with the positive.
- Ask questions and listen to the responses.
- Give specific examples as part of the feedback.
- Make helpful suggestions for improvement.
- Check the student's understanding and agreement.
- Offer help and support.
- Always end on a positive and upbeat note.

- Summarise and agree the next steps; set a timetable for a review.

All these elements are equally valuable skills for young people to develop. Listening effectively, asking questions and giving constructive feedback are important parts of a toolkit for young people.

Setting goals

Helping individual learners achieve something can be supported by setting SMART objectives. Often it is hard to achieve focus. SMART can be used with parents and children together to agree with the teacher what they are going to focus on:

- *Specific.* What exactly does your learner need to achieve? Can they write it in one sentence? If there are several objectives, can you help them prioritise?
- *Measurable.* Exam results are one measure, but there are many more that can be identified before that end result. Often it is exam failure that focuses the mind. SMART could help before that stage. What other measures of success could be identified, e.g. getting course work in on time or completing the assignment in the correct way?
- *Achievable.* This is one of the most important tests of an objective. If it is not achievable then the student is going to become really demotivated and is being set up for failure. Sometimes it is more effective to set bite-sized objectives, to encourage a student to keep going.
- *Realistic.* This is another very important stage. This moves a goal from fantasy to reality. It is no good the learner setting goals that are totally unrealistic. This does not mean that they shouldn't set themselves challenges, or aspire to achieve more, but it is about building for success.
- *Timed.* You can help your student by agreeing realistic time lines. For creative individuals this will be one of their greatest challenges. Struggling to meet deadlines will be something that they are likely to live with all their lives. For many creative people their creativity only kicks in when they are running out of time.

Many students leave assignments to the very last minute and stay up all night to finish. Helping them to identify ways of creating other deadlines to kick-start their work will give them an important skill.

Grow

Another coaching technique is GROW. If you are working with students, this is way of adding structure to the questions in your conversations:

- *Goals:*
  What are your SMART goals?
  What exactly do you want to achieve?
  Why are you hoping to achieve this goal?
  What are the expectations of others?
  Who else needs to know about your plan? How will you inform them?

- *Reality:*
  What is the reality of your current situation?
  Why haven't you reached this goal already?
  What is really stopping you?
  Do you know anyone who has achieved this goal?
  What can you learn from them?

- *Options:*
  What could you do as a first step?
  What else could you do?
  Who do you know who has done it differently?
  What could you learn from them?
  What would happen if you did nothing?

- *Will:*
  Where does this goal fit in with your personal priorities at present?
  Do you have other priorities which are taking your energy and motivation?

What obstacles do you expect to meet? How will you overcome them?

How would you score your level of commitment on a scale of 0–10?

If your commitment score is less than 8, will you actually get started?

Do you really want to do it? If yes, when are you going to start?

(Adapted from John Whitmore, *Coaching for Performance*, 1996 – see 'Recommended reading')

Coaching can be a very valuable approach either to encourage deeper learning in the classroom or one on one.

The teacher as coach

The coaching conversations that are carried out in the classroom are limited by the amount of time, the location and the individuals involved. What is important is trying to create a coaching relationship that is as natural as possible. The coaching behaviours should become embedded in the day-to-day activities within the classroom.

If we think about coaching in the classroom and profile the role, there will be certain behaviours that will identify those individuals who most naturally adapt to the role of coach. These are the attitudes and behaviours that are demonstrated by the very best teachers, and are built on a genuine interest in others.

The best coaches:

- build a positive environment;
- ask questions to analyse needs;
- use open questions to probe;
- focus on the needs of the individual;
- offer suggestions to build on the views expressed by learners;
- listen actively;
- seek ideas and build on them;
- give feedback;
- agree action plans for development;
- monitor performance;
- give ongoing support;

- focus on improving performance;
- assist in raising performance to the required standards;
- emphasise the present.

To develop effectiveness as a coach it is helpful to understand more about how people learn, how people react and adapt to change and what motivates people to want to do things differently. From a personal perspective it is worth identifying and understanding some of the tools and techniques used by coaches that have just been mentioned.

Attributes of good coaches

In addition, good coaches:

- are trusted and respected;
- live the values;
- have relevant experience, which adds value;
- have good communication skills – they question, build, clarify and summarise;
- offer encouragement and support;
- take time to listen;
- let people figure things out for themselves;
- work in partnership;
- have a strong belief that improvement is always possible;
- focus on an end goal;
- take joint responsibility for the outcome.

Code of practice

Coaches often develop a code of practice, which is equally relevant in a teacher's relationship with students:

- Respect confidentiality at all times.
- Offer coaching, not counselling, but recognise when an individual student may need additional support.
- Work to create a supportive and appropriately challenging environment.

- Focus on a holistic view.
- Have the desire to want to model and challenge development.
- Be curious – stimulate curiosity in your learner.
- Recognise that the individual is in charge of their own destiny.

This is only the starting point. Before embarking on a coaching role it is important to think very carefully about what it entails and to identify what you believe is important to include in your own code of practice. As highlighted earlier, coaching behaviours are important for anyone to develop, to self-coach, to peer-coach or in your relationship with students. It is also important, however, to seek support and training for the role. This chapter only highlights key areas to consider. It cannot replace the learning required to become an effective coach.

Self-knowledge

- How well do know yourself?
- Can you accurately describe your strengths and areas of development?
- Do you really understand how you will react in different circumstances?
- Do you listen to advice from other people?
- Have you received feedback that has helped you to gain insight into your personality or the way you react to others?

All teachers can benefit from increasing their self-knowledge. Chapter 11 covers this in more detail.

Key stages in coaching

As part of my research into the role of a coach, I have identified some key stages, which apply equally to being an inspiring teacher.

Creating the climate

This stage relates not just to the initial meeting, but also to subsequent meetings. Often when someone is being coached for the first time they may be unsure what to expect. They may have very limited experience of what it is like to be coached. For the new coach too, particularly if it is in the classroom, the surroundings may not naturally be conducive to creating the right learning environment. However, with experience a good coach can create the feeling of being connected to the learner even in the busiest conditions. What is important is the attention to the individual and the application of coaching behaviours. A good coach needs to help the learner create their vision, and is able to work in partnership with the individual to build an infrastructure to support coaching. They should also be able to contextualise the learning, i.e. help them to develop the right skill in the right context.

Building relationships

The ability to build relationships is at the core of being a good teacher. The need to have enhanced interpersonal skills and to develop emotional intelligence are critical in the development of the role of the teacher. As mentioned earlier, the ability to develop a natural coaching style while at the same time being able to use different interventions can be invaluable. Transferring knowledge while understanding how people learn can make the learning experience much more effective. Structuring the learning so that you take account of the needs of the learner and adapting your style to suit the learner are important stages in building a relationship. Being open and responsive and having a genuine interest in the learner can also help to build a relationship. Using the right interventions at the right time is another important skill to develop. In a coaching relationship a coach is often accompanying a learner on a journey. It may be a journey towards developing a particular skill, it may be a journey towards achieving a particular ambition or it may be the completion of a specific action plan. Tuning in to the learner and identifying how they may be feeling, knowing when to check on progress or simply taking time to talk to them one to one, just to remind them of your support, is an important part of the role of a coach.

There is also another really important ingredient in a good teacher, which really can make the difference between success and failure:

it is the ability to inspire. There may be many moments when as a teacher you doubt your ability to inspire anyone. However, ultimately this is what makes the difference in the coaching relationship. It is the intuitive ability to say the right thing and take the right action which elevates the learner into that ultimate achievement of self-belief.

Open to experience

Although not immediately apparent when thinking about the role of the teacher, this stage is equally important and often is responsible for some of the breakdowns in teacher–student relationships. Everyone is different and has different hopes, dreams and aspirations. One of the reasons why ambitions are sometimes capped is because of the views of others. Teachers, parents and other adults are often responsible for limiting an individual's belief in their ability to achieve something. As highlighted in the stage above, part of the role of the teacher is to be able to inspire the learner and so, when an individual learner is testing out embryonic ideas with a teacher, it is important for the teacher not to make assumptions based on their own experience but to remain open-minded and to listen to the ideas of the learner. This is why it is important for a teacher to understand their own ability to generate ideas and be creative and innovative, and why sometimes there may be a need to identify with the learner other colleagues who may be able to offer alternative suggestions, advice or support. There may also be a need to help the learner reset their assumptions, if their experience to date has resulted in low self-esteem. A teacher acting as a coach can help them challenge and avoid self-fulfilling prophecies of failure.

Solution partner

A teacher acting as a coach needs to be able to rise above the issues, help a learner to work through opportunities and challenges, and act as a sounding board. You may also be offering coaching support to a colleague and, if so, you may be helping them to work towards a solution. It is important to be able to have a mature conversation, offer meaningful advice, use problem-solving tools and techniques, and help the learner, whether a colleague or a student, to generate alternatives or solutions. Another important area is helping the learner to manage risk appropriately. Some learners will be risk-averse, while others may be risk takers; a good coach will encourage the learner to make an accurate risk assessment. Ultimately, however, the decisions will need to be taken by the individual, and they have to own the solution. A coach's role is help them to take steps forward and to support them if they fall back.

Collaborative

Ideally, a good teacher acting as coach can help the student to net-work, suggest other support and contacts, help the learner to make connections and, if they cannot provide the contacts themselves, know someone who can. It is very easy within one-to-one coaching relationships for the focus to remain on either the learner or the coach. However, most individuals are part of a much bigger group of people and helping the learner to make connections with others is an important part of the role of a good teacher. Traditionally, graduates within organisations are given mentors who are often seen as people who could provide high-potential employees with the opportunity to meet contacts as part of their development. However, there is a much more natural process of communication within organisations which can enable people to share ideas, build on the experience of others and work collaboratively on projects. It does need to be stimulated, though, as it is all too easy for people not to share information. A good coach can link people either individually or in teams to share information and best practice inside a school or college.

Appropriate closure and maintaining the relationship

This is an important stage: knowing how to complete conversations. As identified above, timing is everything in a coaching relationship. In a coaching conversation, it is important to understand the point at which to pause or stop and to encourage the learner to go and put their thoughts and discoveries into practice. Often when people find a supportive teacher who is genuinely interested in them, like a thirsty plant they drink up the attention. However, the learning will be more effective if it forms part of a cycle of input, practice and feedback. This stage takes on a new importance in an ongoing relationship where the learner is encouraged to move forward with less coaching support. In any teaching relationship there will come a time when the relationship has run its course and the student is ready to move on, but most people remember the teacher who showed them care and attention. Identifying this point and handling it appropriately is important. There has to be a combination of reassurance, encouragement and inspiration to encourage the learner to move forward.

The teacher as coach profile

Identifying your preferred coaching style can be an important part of your development as a more effective teacher. Here is a sample of statements for you to consider:

- *Create the climate:*
  I am able to create an environment that is conducive to learning.
  I am able to focus on the needs of the learner.
  I am not easily distracted by my surroundings.
  I believe learning can take place anywhere with the right coaching skills.

- *Build relationships:*
  I have taken time to identify my interpersonal skills.
  People have given me positive feedback about the way I interrelate with others.
  I am a good listener.
  I am able to ask questions to determine learning needs.

- *Open to experience:*
  I can rise above the immediate situation and see new opportunities.
  I am not constrained by past experiences.
  I can often encourage learners to take explorative steps forward.
  I can inspire others to look at situations in a new light.

- *Solution partner:*
  Other people often use me as a sounding board for their ideas.
  I can often see new ways of approaching a problem.
  I enjoy working as a partner with others.
  I can encourage others to work through issues constructively.

- *Collaborative:*
  I have a network of professional people that I use to help me achieve my goals.
  Within my organisation I work hard to develop networks and encourage my learners to meet with others.
  I can see the natural linkages between key projects within the organisation.

- *Appropriate closure:*
  When I am working in a coaching relationship I encourage the learners to plan for their future independence.

Right time, right place and right person

In terms of your own learning, some of the most powerful learning will happen when you find the right time, the right place and the right person to guide your personal understanding. These conversations will be very special and may not happen that often, but, when you meet people who are interesting and stimulating, cherish those moments. In those circumstances it is likely that you may experience personal insights which are so profound that the memory will stay with you for ever.

6 'Rage to learn'

Supporting gifted children

In *Gifted Children* (see 'Recommended reading'), Ellen Winner (1997) describes 'exceptionally bright' children as having notable energy and curiosity, and suggests that they have a 'rage to learn'. She suggests that they have their own in-built drivers and that their parents, rather than pushing their children, appear to be pulled along by the sheer momentum of their youngsters' talent or talents.

In order to rediscover their creativity, people often need to relearn and unlearn some of the lessons learnt in childhood. Not everyone responds to a traditional learning environment. This chapter will explore what opportunities exist for children who are gifted and how to create environments that are more inclusive. This chapter will focus on how to support gifted individuals from a position of recognising that all children have a talent but some may need extra support to enable them to make the most of their potential.

Who is that child?

Look at the dishevelled child coming late into your class, jumper half on, glasses held together by sticky tape, ink-stained fingers, hair standing on end, yawning as he takes his place near the front of the classroom. At playtime you know he is either ignored or jeered at by other children. Is he deprived? Does he come from a disadvantaged home? What are his parents thinking of, sending him to school like that? This child isn't deprived, but he is carrying a burden: he is carrying the burden of his own talent. And for many children this is a burden they may carry for the whole of their lives. Talent comes in many forms: some are described as bright and gifted; others are described as dyslexic; others are seen as disruptive; others may go on as adults to be described as 'mavericks'. To be creative or academically gifted, particularly in the arts, carries many challenges; to be a gifted sports person is seen as cool. To be gifted in an artistic or technical talent is often seen as geeky; most children aspire to be a Beckham rather than a Gates.

To return to the child above, the reason why he looks the way he does is because, outside school, he lives in his own world. He either reads late into the night or he is writing his own stories, which he scrawls with a fountain pen and ink in almost indecipherable writing because his hands can barely keep up with his brain. As he has fallen asleep late, his mother has been unable to wake him in the morning; he gets dressed in a dream and, because he is still thinking about his story, he absentmindedly sits on his glasses. In class he is bored. He knows better now than to put his hand up to answer the questions. He learnt that lesson early on; the names that he was called by the other children when he showed enthusiasm have taught him to remain silent like the rest of the class. Yet, just before he goes out to play, he says quietly to you, 'Would you like to borrow the new Stephen King book?'

How can you support a child like this? There are many challenges. First is engaging with the child and recognising the depth and breadth of his talent. Conventional testing may not capture all the dimensions of his talent. Second is encouraging his interest across a broad spectrum of learning. Sometimes gifted children want to focus on only one area and as a result neglect other areas of learning.

Miraca Gross, in *Exceptionally Gifted Children* (2004) (see 'Recommended reading'), introduced 15 very gifted young people and traced their path through school, and then in the second edition of the book followed their path into adulthood.

Gross emphasises the importance of creating a 'sure shelter', somewhere where gifted children feel at home with others:

> It cannot be sufficiently emphasized that the problems of social isolation, peer rejection, loneliness and alienation which afflict many highly gifted children arise not out of their exceptional intellectual abilities but *as a result* of society's response to them.

These problems arise when the school, the education system, or the community refuses to create for the exceptionally gifted child a peer group based not on the accident of chronological age, but on a commonality of abilities, interest and values. Only through the creation of such a group can exceptionally, or profoundly gifted children be freed from the taunts and jeers of age-peers, the pressure to camouflage their abilities in a desperate and futile struggle to conceal their difference, and the frightening sense of being the one-eyed man in the country of the blind who is distrusted and resented because he has vision – or perhaps because of what he can see . . . When it *is* achieved, it colours and transforms one's life.

She quotes from the work of Joyce VanTassel-Baska, who identified five elements which are essential to the success of a programme for gifted students:

1   content acceleration to the level of the child's abilities;
2   thoughtfully planned, relevant enrichment;
3   guidance in selecting courses and directions;
4   instruction with the opportunity to work closely with other gifted young people;
5   the opportunity to work with mentors who have a high level of expertise in the child's area of giftedness.

Howard Gardner, in *Extraordinary Minds* (1997) (see 'Recommended reading'), suggests three major lessons that have emerged from his study of extraordinariness:

1   Extraordinary individuals stand out to the extent to which they reflect – often explicitly – on the events of their lives, large as well as small.
2   Extraordinary individuals are distinguished less by their impressive 'raw powers' than by their ability to identify their strengths and then to exploit them.
3   Extraordinary individuals fail often and sometimes dramatically. Rather than giving up, however, they are challenged to learn from their setbacks and to convert defeats into opportunities.

He also identifies four forms of extraordinariness:

- *A Master.* This is 'an individual who gains complete mastery over one or more domains of accomplishment; his or her innovation occurs within established practice'. In this context he gives Mozart as an example.
- *The Maker.* A Maker 'may have mastered existing domains, but they devote energies to the creation of a new domain'. He suggests Freud as having created the domain of psychoanalysis.
- *An Introspector.* This is 'someone who wants to explore their inner life, their hopes and fears, daily experiences'. In this context he suggests Virginia Woolf and James Joyce.
- *The Influencer.* This person 'has a primary goal of influencing other individuals'. He gives the examples of Gandhi, Karl Marx and Machiavelli.

He suggests that we all possess the potential in some form to occupy each of the roles; we can all master a domain, vary that domain in a significant way, introspect about ourselves and influence others. Equally, he suggests that 'no sharp line divides the form of extraordinariness. Since every action is to some extent original . . . It may be useful to think of our four exemplars arranged in a circular configuration, with each having ties to the other possible stances.'

In his discussion about extraordinariness Gardner suggests that achieving disciplinary or scholarly expertise is not the same as achieving extraordinariness. With good teaching most people are capable of gaining expertise or becoming competent. For most people, he states, achieving expertise in one area is enough: 'it allows us to make a living, fit into a community and raise our children'.

In working with the individual learner it is important that you help them to recognise that who they are will impact on what they want to do and how they are able to achieve their goals.

Being original

Based in the comments above, one way that giftedness may be demonstrated is through originality. In Chapter 4, the Torrance Tests of Creative Thinking (TTCT) were highlighted. One of the measures in those tests is originality. It is important that we encourage children who are trying to express what may seem to be original thought to them. Think about how children learn. In their very early years so much is by discovery, which is their first faltering steps to freedom. For a first or an only child, many of their first discoveries may seem completely unique to them and to their first-time parents too. For many nursery, reception and primary teachers, the learning that takes place in the early years is one of the reasons why they enjoy teaching; no matter how many times teachers experience it, seeing children enjoying learning brings its own rewards.

But what happens as children get older? What happens to their embyronic ideas and their imagination? How much are they encouraged to try and not worry if they fail? How much credence is given to what they believe is original thought? How much encouragement is given to those who don't fit the mould, or are they seen as 'difficult'? A child with natural curiousity may be encouraged in their early years only to be greeted with less enthusiasm as they persist in questioning later in life, both at home and at school. The constant asking of 'Why?' instead of a passive acceptance of 'It just is' is seen as challenging by many, not just parents or teachers, but often other children too; and so often the questions stop, to be replaced by an inner frustration or a desire to get out of school to pursue their real interests in their own time. Yet today many organisations are desperate to be seen as 'thought leaders'. This thought leadership will only come from those people who have the ability to lead the field, discover different perspectives and challenge convention. Therefore it is essential that schools foster originality, innovation and creativity.

How to create an environment to support giftedness

As I have mentioned elsewhere in this book, every child is different, but increasingly it is being recognised that giftedness is something that needs extra support and, as Torrance indicated with his tests, being gifted in creativity may need different support, as such talents may not be recognised in traditional testing. Every child needs intellectual challenge, and this may not necessarily be the same as for their peers. The child who has learnt to read at home does not need to be taken back to the beginning in order to progress at the same pace as their peers. All the techniques mentioned in Chapters 3, 4 and 5 have a relevance to gifted children as well as other children.

What these techniques can do is provide depth to the learning of gifted children. For example, even very young children respond to probing questions. Instead of them asking 'Why?', turn the tables on them and ask them to find the answers. Help them to recognise that learning is a journey of discovery and encourage their parents to be involved too. Sometimes with gifted children the relationship between school and home becomes strained, with the parents unwilling to communicate the real depth and breadth of the talent of their child to the school because they may be seen as boasting. By parents and teachers working together, the gifted child, particularly in pre-school or infant classrooms, can be identified early and given the support that they need.

One of the very real challenges for gifted children can be relationships with their peers, and this is particularly true as they progress through primary and into secondary school. Finding a gifted child in a reception class can be a source of joy to the teacher, but how they respond to this child may have real impact as the child progresses through schooling. There is a sensitive balance between allowing the gifted child to contribute and creating positive relationships with their peers. As mentioned above, other children are often critical of the child who appears to 'know everything'. Giftedness reveals itself in different ways: some children are quiet and withdrawn, others may appear bossy, some really do demonstrate multiple intelligences, but there is no one way that defines gifted behaviour. What is important is that teachers and parents work together in identifying the best way of developing gifted children in both their academic ability and their social and emotional abilities.

Individual support

Gifted children often respond well to adults, as many of their conversations are in advance of those of their peers, but it can be difficult for teachers to give the gifted child the attention that they need within the normal classroom. This is where blended learning can help in allowing the teacher to structure the learning to allow a mix of individual support and challenging activities. In a blended environment, the learning can be tailored to provide the gifted child with the opportunity to quietly progress to much higher levels, being stimulated and challenged by, for example, software designed for older learners.

There is support for teachers working with gifted children. The National Academy for Gifted and Talented Youth (NAGTY) (see contact details in Chapter 12) was set up by the government, at the University of Warwick. NAGTY's remit is to improve gifted and talented education in schools, as well as targeting specific support for the top 5 per cent. It aims to improve provision for gifted and talented children and young people up to the age of 19 years, and to provide guidance, advice and development for teachers. It is the centre of expertise for gifted education in England.

The National Academy's core infrastructure funding comes from the DfES, with additional funding generated through successful partnerships with businesses, charitable trusts and individuals.

Recently it has been given the lead responsibility for the creation and development of a national register for England's gifted and talented children. The national register will seek to identify all gifted and talented learners using the full range of measures available to schools and colleges, as exemplified in NAGTY's admissions process. It will also help schools to track the progress of their gifted and talented learners, as well as targeting appropriate learning and development opportunities.

In addition, increasingly within many schools there is additional support through specialist teachers with responsibility for gifted and talented children.

Inclusion

There has to be a balance between giving gifted children the intellectual support that they need and the social and interpersonal development to help them integrate in the classroom. Some gifted children's behaviour can alienate them from their peers, and as a result they may either withdraw from contributing or become the victims of bullying or ridicule from others. As Gross mentioned, creating a 'sure shelter' for gifted children can be very important for their development. Part of this may consist of identifying additional opportunities for gifted children to attend events with other gifted children; for example, NAGTY run special events that gifted children can attend. In addition, there may be the opportunity within the school for small group work or special projects which allow gifted children to explore their potential with other gifted children.

Much of the success of this will depend on the ability of the teacher to create an environment where learning is seen as stimulating, challenging and fun and where all children are encouraged to push themselves and to fulfil their potential. Coombes School (see Chapter 4) is such an example, as is Writhlington School (see Chapter 9). In both these schools, individual teachers have, through their own passion and commitment, pushed the boundaries of the curriculum to create learning experiences which are stimulating and exciting for all children, but which will allow the gifted child to explore to the limit of their capabilities.

Transitional stages

As discussed above, it is important to maintain school-to-home links, but it is also important to support gifted children as they make moves between classes at school and from one school to the next. For the gifted child who has been encouraged through nursery and infant schools, moving to a more structured primary school and then to secondary school can result in a reduction in their creativity at each transitional stage.

As has also been indicated above, this may manifest itself in many ways: it may be in their willingness to contribute, it may be in their actual work or it may be in a reluctance to attend school. Gifted children and young adults more than most suffer through a sense of being misunderstood.

If we look at the responses in the next section and the comments from creative adults given in Chapter 2, it is clear that many children do not want to be seen as being different; therefore as they progress through the school system they learn to 'dumb down' their talents. Equally, others who do not want a generalist education or are less confident in other subjects, as they move through the system, may lose or reduce their belief in their ability to be intuitively creative. This also applies to students making the transition from school to university, and from university to the world of work. This is covered in more detail in Chapter 9, but helping gifted young people identify what they want to do with the rest of their lives is highly significant.

As Gardner (1997) states, it's the complexity of what a gifted child can contribute that is the challenge for them. The overwhelming response from many of the adult mavericks interviewed is that organisations on the whole just do not know how to get the best from them, nor are the organisations able to create environments that allow these adults to make the contribution that they are really capable of giving. Helping young people to select the right university and employer, and educating employers about the contribution that gifted students can make is a challenge for all educators.

In my background research with creative and talented adults I asked them about their experiences of school. Here are some of the findings.

Experiences of school

> I found school to be easy although always related to older pupils in primary and junior schools. I went to a top 2 per cent selective grammar school so was always in a competitive environment where I was in the top 25 per cent of class.

> A good 11-plus result and encouragement from my parents meant that, instead of joining my friends at the local secondary modern, I arrived with three others from my primary school at the local boys grammar. I remember having five fights on my first day and not starting any of them. I learnt that punishments from schoolmasters were preferable to being bullied by my classmates and I learnt how to do just enough to get by and not stand out for any reason. Looking back the best that came from my school years was the experience of being immersed in an 'alien' environment and the opportunity it gave me to learn how to fit into it until I could leave.

Positive. Represented high school at multiple sports at a state level. Played multiple sports at the same time. Didn't do as well at studying until I went to university. This is where I seemed to excel and then into postgraduate studies.

I enjoyed school, but regularly got told off for chatting or daydreaming – so maybe these are true skills of the 'talented', but I'm not sure how they can be nurtured at school with all the academic subjects children have to get results in nowadays. I also learnt things very quickly except for spelling and maths!

Experiences OK. If my talent is writing stories, then sometimes this was supported and other times not. In order to be good at anything, it takes a lot of time and dedication and I started doing this at an early age, but the UK school system is not really designed to teach someone how to be good at one thing. It aims instead for a balanced education.

I loved prep school and the whole environment. I had no confidence at public school, an event that was a disaster.

How old were you when you thought you might be talented?

I never actually thought I was talented but from primary school knew I was different.

I never regarded myself as talented until my mid-thirties, although I did spend periods of my childhood feeling different from other kids around me. I think I was more sensitive and aware than most of the children I grew up with and this was equally true regarding some of the adults in my neighbourhood. I tended to distance myself and observe others until I'd learnt to blend in. Sometimes it felt good to be different, but more often as a child I felt uncomfortable about not being like others.

About 15.

Still not sure I am talented. Or at least what 'talent' is. I have certain skills, which taken together might be seen as a talent.

Five years old when I won a ballet award and although the teacher raved about my ability as a dancer I just wanted to try something else and see how successful I could be at that. As I got older I applied myself to all sorts of things – gymnastics, art, play writing – and the same thing happened: a little application seemed to get me great praise. This, I think, instilled a core belief in me that 'I can do anything I really want to do.'

Ten years old when I started coming top in my class at school.

Firstly, I should say that until I was maybe 20 I was under the belief that I had no talent, none whatsoever, none in any field, and was never encouraged by the teachers in the comprehensive school system (which I blame for the situation) and cannot ever recall being praised by teachers, by my father (and my mum was encouraging but lacked the practical understanding to know whether I was doing well at whatever I was doing). I was therefore under the belief that I was decidedly below average or worse, and that the streaming in comp schools exacerbated that notion. For example, in my third year I was in class 3U which we all called 3Useless (and we were the second highest of eight streams!).

Later when I was doing O level human biology and the then curriculum allowed the class to be taught by one teacher who then had the prerogative, towards the end of the year, to decide whether the county authorities would pay for you to sit the GCE or the CSE, not that they ever were regarded as one being better than the other (ha bloody ha). And the teacher said that I would only be put in for the CSE.

I was furious, and KNEW I could do the GCE, and because my mum had no money (our electric had been cut off and we were literally living off corn flakes for breakfast and dinner) and so I saved up and put five weeks' paper-round money into me paying for the exam. It was £32 in 1969, and as a 15-year-old I had to get up at 5.30 a.m. for 30 days on the trot to pay for it.

I passed both CSE at Grade 1 and GCE at Grade B. My V-sign to the teachers was so, so big! Is that talent recognition or high-mindedness? I don't know!

I guess I was 22, 23 when I realised that I had some talent, not necessarily O level-type talent (I guess I had always been led to believe that O levels or taught subjects were the benchmark of talent) but talents that might be less academic, and outside of what was on the school curriculum.

There is *no one* without talent, and it was running YTS/YT that made me discover that. It was merely that the right key to the door hadn't been found and that the door hadn't been opened. Young, Thick and Stupid, YTS – no way! Only Young, Thick and Stupid when the teachers hadn't got to open their doors!

Discretionary contribution

One of their biggest challenges for talented adults is trying to manage their creativity, both in terms of when it happens and also in terms of the sheer volume of ideas, passions and genuine enthusiasm. Helping them to identify which ideas are worth pursuing, finding other ways of progressing ideas that they have lost interest in, and helping them integrate with others are just some of the issues for people working with talented adults. One model that I have developed is about discretionary contribution, which applies equally well to gifted children. It is based on five levels and is similar to Maslow's theory of motivation and his hierarchy of needs.

Model of discretionary contribution

1   *Willingness to attend.* This first stage is based on an assumption that individuals, once recruited, are willing to attend your organisation. At this stage their drivers may very much be based on the sentiment 'It's a job.' They will have very little loyalty and may not yet feel very engaged with the organisation. For gifted children attending school this can be a very similar feeling: 'Do I have to go to school? I don't learn anything there.'

2   *Willingness to contribute.* At this stage the individual, as well as entering through the gates of your organisation, is willing to make a contribution. How they continue to make that contribu-

tion will very much depend on the expectations of their performance, how successful they feel they are and the feedback that they receive. For the gifted child, as mentioned above, their willingness to contribute will depend on the classroom environment that they find themselves in. Initially they may over-contribute, always being first with the answer, but then they usually realise that this is alienating their classmates and so gradually they withdraw their contribution.

3 *Willingness to work with others.* Assuming that they are successful and depending on the encouragement they receive and the impact of other team members on them, they start interacting, one hopes positively, with others. For the gifted child this is one area where they may often struggle. In the playground the gifted child may be the one standing by the teacher, perhaps talking animatedly because this is one time when they get the attention of an adult, or they may be the one standing on their own. In classroom activities, they may be the one who is last to be picked in team games, or where they have been successfully integrated they may work with other members of the class where their contribution is recognised and valued.

4 *Willingness to lead others.* Over a period of time they may demonstrate leadership qualities, which provides them with an opportunity to progress. This may mean more money, but it may also mean leaving familiar work and team-mates behind. Some choose this route; others refuse this opportunity. Talented people sometimes do not want responsibility for others. The more creative and 'maverick' individuals rarely want to manage others; they find it hard enough managing themselves. This applies to gifted children too. At an early age some gifted children enjoy being the leader. Sometimes this comes across as 'being bossy' or they may genuinely care for their peers and seek to lead them into interesting adventures. As they get older this can translate into anti-social behaviour when they have too much time on their hands or their imagination gets carried away, or equally they may enjoy leading projects. As with the adult mavericks, others may prefer more solitary activities.

5 *Willingness to make a discretionary contribution.* At this stage individuals go beyond their required contribution to offer a

discretionary contribution. The assumption is that people in this zone recognise the contribution that they make in their normal day-to-day work, but they also choose to offer more than is required. This may include volunteering, working extra time on a project, thinking about ideas outside of work, and willingness to represent the company externally. Above all, it is an attitude of mind which engages with the heart and soul, and an employee is prepared to go the extra mile for an organisation. Many SMEs' successes are built on discretionary activity. This equally applies to well-adjusted gifted children who find themselves in an environment which supports them, integrates them and allows them to excel; in this context there is no limit to what a gifted child will contribute.

Finally, here is checklist in how to help support gifted children:

- Be genuinely interested in *all* children, but be prepared to recognise the additional support that gifted children need. Use external resources such as NAGTY and internal school resources where they exist to offer specialist support.
- Recognise giftedness early, and acknowledge that it can take many forms.
- Support gifted children through key transition stages; work with parents and teacher colleagues to ensure that the children are supported through the transition.
- Motivate all children by tapping into their interests and passions. Enthuse them with your own energy. Spend time with them. Show a genuine interest in them and their interests.
- Identify and develop content that is stretching, incremental and suitably challenging.
- Maintain close contact with parents, particularly in the early years, to understand the scale and scope of the giftedness.
- Provide opportunities for gifted children to work with other gifted children. As appropriate, identify other adults who could act as mentors.
- Give children recognition, show you value them and encourage them to take responsibility. Monitor them and give them constructive feedback on their performance.

- Provide sensitive support to help them integrate with others. Recognise their giftedness, but encourage them to recognise the different talents of their peers.

Most of us are content to engage in what might be termed 'little e' extraordinariness – perhaps dabbling in the writing of a poem, or a story. Only a few individuals have the talent and the nerve to reach for the stars – to seek to attain 'the big E' Extraordinariness, where their contributions actually help to reconfigure a significant realm of human experience. These people may have to assume ever-increasing responsibilities in the brave new worlds to come.

(Howard Gardner, *Extraordinary Minds*, 1997)

7 Building self-esteem

'Hope fires a neuron.' Certain quotes stay in your mind and take on a life of their own. I first read this in Ian Gilbert's *Essential Motivation in the Classroom* (2002) (see 'Recommended reading'). Gilbert first heard it quoted by Professor John MacBeath from Strathclyde University; he didn't think that it was original to him. Gilbert goes on to describe how, when we are in a state of hopefulness, 'our brains literally light up with electrical energy coursing around the upper-intellectual regions'. However, by contrast, when we are in a state of hopelessness 'the brain will dim with the energy downshifting . . . to the lower, more basic, do-the-bare-minimum-to-survive elements'.

He then goes on to describe students' brains by saying:

> Imagine your students' crania are transparent and that when you are working with them you can see the electrical activity flashing around their heads. Watch as your positive comment, 'You'll go far', or a rewarding look, or little nudge simply lights up their brain.
>
> Alternatively, watch as you chase away all hope with your disparaging comments. 'Maths isn't really your thing is it?' 'I don't think you'll make it as a poet.' 'Call that a sheep?'

Paul Torrance had a similar view quoted in *The Career Guide for Creative and Unconventional People* (Eikleberry, 1999): 'Society is downright savage to creative thinkers especially when they are young.'

Are you a hope giver or a hope taker? Do your students walk away from your classroom with higher levels of hope and optimism than when they walk in?

Building self-esteem

Many adults still suffer from the negative impact of their schooling; this chapter really explores ways in which children can be encouraged to build inner resilience and self-belief.

We mentioned self-belief in Chapter 4, and the power of positive thinking. National sports teams, businesses and individuals are continually being encouraged to develop self-belief; therefore isn't the most logical place to start with the younger generation?

There is a strong belief by the writers of many personal development and self-help books that if you really believe in something you can make it happen; it is the power of positive thought. Another way of describing it is 'self-talk'. Shad Helmstetter in *What to Say when You Talk to Yourself* (1998) argues powerfully about the need to programme your brain into positive thoughts rather than the negative messages that we receive in our lives.

One of the sad realities is that many people underachieve, often as a result of the feedback that they receive from others. Parents, teachers, friends and partners are often responsible for giving (often unsolicited) advice or feedback which so undermines an individual's confidence that they give up on a plan or course of action because of doubts fuelled by someone else. What this often does is to reinforce the concerns that they may already have.

Helmstetter says that leading behavioural researchers have told us that as much as '77% of everything we think is negative and counterproductive and works against us'. He then asks:

> What if each and every day, from the time you were a small child, you had been given an extra helping of self-confidence, double the amount of determination, and twice the amount of belief in the outcome? Can you imagine what tasks you might accomplish more easily, what problems you would overcome, what goals you would reach? . . . Could it be that those who appear to be 'luckier' than the rest have only gotten a little better programming? . . . It is no

longer a success theory . . . The brain simply believes what you tell it most.

Closely related to self-confidence is what psychologists call 'self-efficacy', the positive judgement of one's own capacity to perform. Self-efficacy is not the same as the actual skills we have, but rather our belief about what we can do with the skills we have. Skill alone is not enough to guarantee our best performance – we have to *believe* in our skills in order to use them at their best. Goleman, in *Working with Emotional Intelligence* (1998) (see 'Recommended reading'), quotes from the work of Albert Bandura, a Stanford University psychologist who pioneered the study of self-efficacy, who points out the contrast between those who doubt themselves and those who believe in their abilities when it comes to taking on a difficult task.

Those with self-efficacy gladly step up to take the challenge; those with self-doubt don't even try, regardless of how well they might actually do. Self-confidence raises expectations and raises aspirations, while self-doubt lowers them. Goleman goes on to state that 'there is a tight link between self-knowledge and self-confidence. We each have an inner map of our proclivities, abilities and deficiencies.' He quotes from two studies:

> In a decades long study of managers at AT&T, self-confidence early in a person's career predicted promotions and success in higher management years later. And in a sixty year study of more than a thousand high IQ men and women followed from child-hood through retirement, those most self-confident in their early years were most successful as their careers unfolded.

Brian Tracy in *Maximum Achievement* (1993) takes a similar line:

> Children who learn to build and maintain their own levels of self-esteem have far better self-concepts than children who do not. Children with high, positive self-concepts do well in school. They do not engage in vandalism, or get into trouble. They don't do destructive things to their bodies. They are more capable of resisting the negative influences of their peer groups. They have stronger characters.

Children with high self-concepts, high self-esteem are independent in their thinking. They are more likely to think for themselves, and to orient themselves toward success, achievement and personal fulfilment. They are more focused on realizing their potential than on compensating for their deficiencies.

He also suggests that, when children feel good about themselves, they develop better judgement about the things that are good for them in the long run. They develop the ability to delay gratification in the short term in order to enjoy greater rewards in the future.

So how do you help children develop a positive self-concept? In reality this is not something that teachers can achieve on their own; it has to be part of a relationship between the child, the parents and the teacher. However, by understanding it and reinforcing the principles you can play a major role in helping a child to develop it. Tracy suggests that a self-concept is made up of three parts:

- *Self-ideal*. He suggests that a person's self-ideal is a vision or an ideal description of the person that someone would most like to be. This may be a combination of values, qualities and attributes and sets the standards for an individual.
- *Self-image*. Again Tracy's view is that your self-image is the way that you see yourself and what you think about yourself and how you go about your daily duties. He describes this as your 'inner mirror' and suggests that you 'always behave consistently with the picture that you hold of yourself on the inside'. Powerfully, he suggests that it is possible to improve one's performance by changing the mental pictures that you hold about yourself in that area. I referred to the work of performance coaches at the start of this chapter, and much of their work is in the area of helping individuals to visualise a more successful person. As people begin to see themselves as becoming more confident and, importantly, as winners, their behaviour becomes more focused and confident. This also links to the visualisation techniques used in Chapter 4.
- *Self-esteem*. The third part of the self-concept is self-esteem. Tracy describes this as 'the source of energy, enthusiasm, vitality

and optimism that powers your personality and makes you a high achieving man or woman'. He suggests that your level of self-esteem is determined by two factors: how valuable and worthwhile you feel you are and how much you like and accept yourself as a good person; and your feeling of 'self-efficacy', as described by Goleman. He suggests that the two sides of your self-esteem reinforce each other. When you feel good about yourself, you perform better, and when you perform well you feel good about yourself.

He sums this up by suggesting that the best measure of self-esteem is how much you like yourself, and states:

> The more you like yourself, the better you do at everything you put your mind to. The more you like yourself, the more confidence you have, the more positive is your attitude, the healthier and more energetic you are and the happier you are overall.

This has enormous implications for teachers and parents. Children are not born with a self-concept; it is developed through interactions and feedback from the adults in their world.

Paradigm shift

As well as the techniques mentioned in Chapter 4, another useful technique is paradigm shift. The logic behind paradigm shift is that you are helping people to make a mindset change. By encouraging a shift from a negative to a positive perspective you are helping them work to achieve what they really want. It builds on the principles of visualisation: visualising what it could be like and then moving further forward into identifying how it could feel. It can range from quite basic human activities like getting up in the morning to the more personal and aspiring, e.g. 'I want to be successful in achieving what I want from life.'

By shifting their personal perspective from disbelief to belief the individual learner can start to work to achieve what they really want. The real issue is that it is easy to say, but much harder to achieve. The role of the teacher as coach can be to help the individual to keep reaffirming their beliefs, help them to identify strategies for achieving the shift and reinforce their embryonic steps towards achieving the reality:

- 'I want to get up easily in the morning – I enjoy getting out of bed and the beauty of mornings.'
- 'I want to be fit and healthy – I am a fit and healthy person.'
- 'I want to be able to network with confidence – people will find me interesting and stimulating.'
- 'I want to achieve my ambition – I have already started and am going to achieve it.'

In each case the first step towards achieving a mindset change is to begin to live as if the shift had already taken place. If I want to get up easily in the morning, what do I need to do to shift my perception of what enjoying getting up feels like? How could I make the mornings a more pleasant experience?

If I want to be more interesting and stimulating, how would it feel to be this person? What behaviours do I need to display? Importantly, as discussed in Chapter 4, this will not be achieved overnight, but the first step is helping a student believe that it is possible. Inviting in speakers who have overcome self-doubt, sharing case studies of people who have overcome adversity, and also giving each individual student time and support and positive feedback can help them take their first tentative steps forward. It is also important to maintain this support and to keep supporting them when they falter on the way or when they reject help. We discuss this more when we examine brand Me in Chapter 9.

Helping individuals to believe in themselves

Building on from the concept of 'paradigm shift', one of the most important acts that an adult can do for a child is to build their self-belief. From the moment that a child is born, the feedback that they receive defines their perception of what they can and cannot do. As adults we cannot and must not limit another person's belief by our own views on what is achievable. There are specific actions that we can do to help young people develop self-belief:

- Believe that each child is different, that they have their own unique combination of intelligences, learning abilities, hopes and desires and, therefore, do not judge them by other children. This particularly applies to younger siblings, who often suffer as a result of the expectations of the similarity, or not, to the their older brothers or sisters.
- Be committed to supporting their development through positive feedback. Remember the quote from Thomas Edison, 'I haven't failed; I have just found 10,000 ways that won't work.'
- Help children build a positive mindset. The body responds to the messages that are sent from the mind. The way someone stands, the speed that they move and the way they respond to the environment around them are based on the messages that their mind sends them. Don't just tell them about a paradigm shift; help them live it each day. Think of all the messages that a child receives each day from family, peers and school; encourage them to develop their own filter.
- Help them to overcome failure. This is particularly true at examination time. Have positive examples of people who have failed and how successful they have become in their own field.
- Remind them that tomorrow is a new day. However hard a particular day has been, however hard life has been, none of us can predict what will happen tomorrow, so encourage them to see it as an opportunity to start afresh, taking with them the wisdom from the past, but with new hope for the future.

How to develop others

As well as the techniques mentioned in this chapter and in Chapters 4 and 5, there are a number of practical day-to-day actions you can take to help children of all ages develop:

- Help them to help themselves.
- Provide a stimulating learning environment.
- Keep a sense of FUN about learning and life.
- Be optimistic and give them a sense of hope in their future.
- Treat each child as an individual.
- Draw the best out of each child.

- Recognise their natural talents and be encouraging.
- Provide a support system.
- Do not hold back creative students; take pride in developing them. Encourage their involvement in different projects.
- Champion and be willing to promote the ideas of students and help them to build new skills by building from small to greater responsibilities.
- Be prepared to share your expertise. Help students to succeed by giving positive and constructive feedback. Seek feedback on your effectiveness.
- Encourage students to build personal development plans, and clearly identify with them their strengths and development areas. Work to create opportunities for them to develop new understanding of their personal capabilities.
- Offer ongoing support and additional learning and coaching opportunities.
- When they leave your class, maintain an interest in their development.
- Invite into school or college role models who can track their journey, people who are more maverick, people who have followed non-traditional roles and people who have overcome adversity.
- Don't see it just as a one-off activity; it needs to be ongoing.

You may want to ask yourself:

- What do I know about me which could impact on the way I help others develop their self-esteem?
- Do I regularly demonstrate to my students my belief in their capability and potential?
- Do I encourage them to create their own positive self-image?
- Do I provide opportunities for all students to perform at their best and work to the limits of their abilities?
- Do I give positive feedback before identifying areas for improvement?
- Have I eliminated all forms of destructive criticism from my conversations with students?

- How could I modify, change or develop my behaviour in order to encourage and develop others? Who do I know who is a good role model?
- How could we improve the school management processes we use to help our students develop more self-esteem?
- What do I need to learn in order to help others learn and develop?

Be a teacher who makes a difference. Take time to get to know the children you teach as individuals. Nurture, respect and value each student and watch those students grow.

8 Creativity and blended learning

Younger people are more comfortable with technology than with a person.

(Jeffrey P. Luker of Andersen Consulting, quoted in Tom Peters, *The Circle of Innovation*, 1997)

If a teacher from the last century wandered into some classrooms today they would marvel at the range of technical equipment available to children and young students. As we all know, the rate of technological advance has been amazing. It is hard to believe that the World Wide Web was only invented by Tim Berners-Lee in 1989, and Google by Larry Page and Sergey Brin in 1995, yet today both these systems are used by millions every day. And it's not just computers. There have been rapid advances in cameras, phones and music systems. Young people carry around in their hands an iPod containing as much music as their parents would have had in their whole record collection, while their great-grandparents thought winding up the handle on a gramophone and playing a record with a scratchy needle was an exciting advance in technology.

With the rapid advances, however, it is hard to keep pace with the latest developments, and there are very real questions about what a school should invest in. It is not appropriate within this book to go into detail about the various options, but what I have done is to highlight some further sources of information in Chapter 12. This chapter instead highlights developing creativity within the broader context of blended learning.

What is blended learning?

'Blended learning' as a term is relatively new, but given the advance of technology it represents one of the most logical and natural evolutions of a learning agenda. It presents an elegant solution to the challenges of tailoring learning and development to the needs of individuals. It also represents an opportunity to integrate the innovative and technological advances offered by online learning with the interaction and participation offered in the best of traditional learning. It is most effective when it is enhanced by using the wisdom and support of teachers.

The active creation of blended learning solutions has varied across the education landscape. While some schools have embraced it and the potential it offers, others have been slower to respond. The 2006 British Educational Communications and Technology Agency (Becta) Review press release states, however, that there has been:

> noticeable progress in engagement with technology in education. Computer stocks in schools and colleges have increased, and there is faster connectivity and access to the internet. In the school sector there is evidence of a rapid growth and adoption and use of whole-class display and other supporting technologies.

The Review also suggests that:

> mobile technologies are set to play an increasing role in education, with personal ownership of laptops and mobile phones on the increase. There has also been an acceleration in the use of ICT by practitioners, especially in schools where it has become increasingly the norm for practitioners to prepare and deliver lessons, using digital resources.

However, the Review also states that 'In particular variations in institutional readiness and capability must be overcome if the education sector is to achieve maximum value from technology investment.'

Blended learning is a mix of:

- multimedia technology;
- CD-ROMs and DVDs;

- virtual classrooms;
- instant messaging, discussion boards and blogs;
- voicemail, email and conference calls;
- online text animation and video-streaming;
- digital cameras, iPods, podcasting, PDAs and mobile phones; and
- traditional forms of classroom training and one-to-one coaching.

Why is blended learning important?

The real importance and significance of blended learning lie in its potential. If we forget the title and focus on the process, blended learning represents a real opportunity to create learning experiences which can provide the right learning at the right time and in the right place for each and every individual, in schools and universities and at home. As I am writing this there is a headline report on the national news of a university lecturer recording his lecture as a podcast so that his students can listen to it at home rather than come to a lecture hall. Blended learning can be truly universal, crossing global boundaries and bringing groups of learners together through different cultures and time zones. In this context, blended learning could become one of the most significant developments of the twenty-first century.

Blended learning represents a very real step towards doing it differently and providing schools, colleges and universities with an opportunity to make progress in ways of working or the environment, or in giving individuals freedom to be themselves. It also encourages collaboration, allowing both students and teachers to extend beyond the confines of the school building. It can open up the world to the learner. Even more importantly, it prepares young people for a world of work where technology is equally important, and provides the potential of new career opportunities for savvy young technologists. It can also link school, home and the local community, and different media can be used to share information from the school to parents.

If you are working as a school to create blended learning, it is important that you explore all the options open to you, but also that you help each other to open your eyes so that you see things that you normally might ignore. Encourage each other to be curious, to have an openness and desire to find out more. In today's society more than ever before, there is a critical need for knowledge management. With the advent of the internet and the speed of technological development, it makes it even more relevant to have some kind of mechanism to help you sift and identify what is important and relevant and what to ignore. Just like the saying 'You don't know what you don't know', you can waste vast amounts of time searching for what you think you might find.

Storyboards and flowcharts

When designing learning events that involve a technological application there is often a need to create flowcharts or storyboards which act as a route map showing the key stages and the progression through the learning. There are also authoring tools that are being developed all the time. The key function of whatever tool or technique is used is to ensure that, where appropriate, the logical sequence of the learning is captured. As with any journey, there may also be stopping-off points where the learner will be encouraged to ask for guidance or to explore concepts, but it is important that an overall map exists. This will relate to a bigger development plan if you are creating an ambitious internal learning environment, or just the key stages on a particular journey.

In very real and practical terms, a flowchart, storyboard or map can be used not only to explain the flow and key steps to web designers or other multimedia producers but usually also as a visual tool to illustrate to the internal team or external providers the route map of the overall development. The need to strip out irrelevant information and define the key steps is a valuable learning lesson for everyone. Taking simple, straightforward steps in a learning process is one of the key benefits of any blended learning solution. Achieving fluency may initially seem challenging, but in blended learning no assumptions can be made. Everything has to be defined with absolute clarity.

Identifying online learning

The principles behind identifying online learning are no different from those of any other learning intervention. As highlighted in

Chapter 3, everyone has particular preferences when learning. In designing the learning experience it is important to take account of these preferences and build a learning experience that provides enough variety to cater for this. The very nature of how we learn means that online learning can only ever be one part of a broader learning experience. Thinking creatively about the design, however, can mean that it can be stimulating, interesting and intimate for the learner.

Who should be designing the materials?

One really important consideration must be how to develop the materials. Although it may be challenging and interesting to develop web-design skills in order to develop your own online materials, it may not be practical or possible within your time-frame of introducing blended learning. Almost every day new material is becoming available as classroom resources, and a critical role for the teacher is staying abreast of these developments and identifying what is relevant and, even more importantly, what represents best practice. Blending external resources into the curriculum is very much the role of the teacher, as is identifying creative ways of using the technology.

Auditing content

Auditing and identifying where relevant content is located within an organisation are highly pertinent. Benchmarking best practice externally and networking with fellow professionals are also important tasks. In this context nothing can replace being linked into local networks and national organisations where materials are evaluated and approved by experts in the field. Assembling a team of sample users to pilot and test the material can be a major contribution to the final success of the product.

Equally, introducing the concept of blended learning to colleagues and to the rest of the organisation can help to ensure that the implementation is more successful.

Design principles

What the online component of blended learning shouldn't be is flat text simply put up on to the web. Used properly, there are excellent opportunities to make learning interactive, dynamic and fun, but it does require the use of specialist design software and IT skills to create an effective learning environment.

There are some important criteria to remember when developing online learning; you can also use this as a checklist for evaluating material developed by others.

It is important to recognise the following:

* Content should be high-quality and interesting.
* Less equals more. Remember that your learner will potentially be reading off a screen.
* Think about print options. Some information can be printed off to read, rather than scrolling through a screen.
* Use a journalistic, conversational style rather than an academic approach.
* You can refer students on to other sites, for articles or resources.
* Ideally, use a designer to enhance your words on-screen.
* Recognise that many students may be viewing material on laptops or smaller screens.
* Select products that make careful use of illustration and animation.
* Remember that, unlike learners using some other forms of learning where the sequence may be more controlled, online learners may be entering a screen in a more random sequence. They may also drill down, so having clear forms of navigation will be important to help them find their way around.

As with the early days of video when people were coming to terms with the ability to photograph people moving, recognise the reason why you are using online learning. It should be giving the learner a richer experience than simply reading flat text. If all that you give them is flat text, however well created, there is a question as to whether this is the best way of presenting the information. Equally, if you select products which are overfull with animation or illustration your learner may simply find it a distraction.

Contract with the learner

One of the benefits of an online environment is that it can create an intimacy with the learner, which needs to be respected. One of the issues with e-commerce has been a very natural reluctance on the part of the user in giving personal information when undertaking a transaction, and learning is no different. Once a user has started a process of interaction, they may be revealing information about themselves which should be protected and treated with integrity. The very nature of the learning that they are undertaking may include them recording their personal responses to different situations; they may be undertaking assessments and they may be sharing their views with others. The following checklist highlights some key areas.

Checklist

Does the learning environment that we have created:

- treat the learner with respect, clarifying what information is confidential and what may be shared with other users, e.g. surveys, norm data, shared discussions?
- seek to engage the learner in an experience which is relevant, inspiring, fun and different?
- encourage the learner to take responsibility for their own learning through carefully planned stages of developing personal ownership?
- provide learning experiences that are stimulating and interesting, and use the right medium for the learning, rather than technology for its own sake?
- use language which is jargon-free, clear and engaging to the learner?
- make the connections between offline and online learning and the classroom environment, so that the learner is able to put the learning into practice?

- provide opportunities for assessment which are valid, reliable and meaningful?
- build opportunities and capacity for online discussion with others in a safe and secure environment?
- encourage the learner to take action and invite feedback from their peers and others?
- offer the right level of support, from prompt technical support through to one-to-one coaching as appropriate?

Implementation checklist

- Have we raised awareness of the learning potential?
- Have we planned the launch of blended learning with the right level of technical and offline support to help with the first few weeks of implementation?
- Have we tested or run a pilot of the materials?
- Do we have back-up technical support to ensure the smooth running of the launch?
- Have we trained the staff in the use and potential of blended learning?

Using other media

As well as online learning there are now many other forms of technology-based classroom learning, and in every case the question must be asked 'Why are we doing this?' Identifying the learning rationale behind the activity is critical. It also is important that the technology is appropriate to the age group. Some forms of activity take longer to achieve any real output and so this needs to be evaluated against the value of the activity in the first place. It also will need careful preparation and, as with any technical equipment, a dry run may be a valuable exercise to make sure that you are confident with the equipment. If it is at all possible, having a second person in to support may also be valuable. There is nothing worse, having raised children's expectations about an exciting interactive lesson, than to be unable to get the equipment to operate. Many schools are also recognising the experience and familiarity of the children or students with the equipment they or their parents own. The equipment also does not need to be particularly sophisticated. Video and digital camera work can be a great starting point for creative projects. However, then progressing to animation can generate great excitement for the children as well as the teachers.

World Wide Wonderment

Love it or hate it, the World Wide Web is a fantastic resource. Of course, it has its critics, particularly when teachers have suffered the results of downloaded answers. However, disciplined searching can be very useful. Using a search engine to gather knowledge in the same way as you would use research in a library brings immediate access to so much global information. Sometimes this can yield too much, but for speed of access and opportunities to explore the world, to ask questions and to network globally it cannot be overestimated. For the creative child it can open up a world which helps to both stimulate and satisfy their natural curiosity. For the teacher or lecturer there is a constant source of research findings and, equally, the opportunity to network with teacher colleagues around the world. There are numerous websites that have been specifically developed for schoolchildren or teachers, a number of which are listed in Chapter 12. One such source is the BBC, which through its Blast website offers teenagers a whole range of creative options through use of film, music, creative writing, art and dance.

Training

One way of learning how to do something has always been to jump in with both feet and start experimenting. However, it will be much more effective if you experiment with someone sitting alongside you sharing the mysteries of the technology. It will also speed up the process of learning to receive proper training about how to maximise the potential of the equipment or the creative learning opportunities. There are opportunities for training offered by both Apple and Microsoft as well as other providers, and national support bodies hold regular conferences. Internally, it can also add value if one person sponsors ICT development and undertakes to keep the rest of the school or college informed of new initiatives. In many schools and colleges this will be a designated responsibility, but, in the absence of that, someone who is enthusiastic and interested can help sift through the deluge of information that arrives for what is relevant and important.

Other key points to remember

One of the disadvantages with the growth of more technology-based learning can be the lack of human contact. Individual learners may be losing the opportunity to talk through their embryonic ideas with other students or their teacher. The whole philosophy of self-managed learning provides individuals with choices about how and where they learn, which has distinct advantages for both the individual and the organisation. However, one of the potential losses from the reduction in teacher-led activity relates not so much to what happens in the classroom or lecture theatre but to what happens to the learning which takes place when an interested adult notices when you are struggling and offers additional support or inspires your interest because of the passion in their teaching. Therefore when introducing blended learning it is important to remember the need still to include opportunities for this level of personal contact as part of the learning experience.

Working virtually

One of the distinct advantages of the new technology is the ability to transmit messages rapidly around the world. One way that this can help in the design of learning is that designers do not need to be in the same location. As well as the application of this globally, it can also apply more locally. What this achieves is a number of things. People working in different areas can potentially add their own suggestions, but also it serves as a valuable communication tool. This same process can be used to share information with others using email or intranets; there are a number of advantages to this, particularly for lecturers or students who may be working on research projects:

1   It allows for the natural and creative development of ideas.

2   A number of people can contribute at the same time.
3   Through use of simple techniques, ideas can be commented upon, amended or added to, while retaining the original document.
4   It is possible to work through different time zones and shorten the development time.
5   Working in this way can help to forge global links and overcome cultural differences.
6   Everyone can work at a time, place and pace to suit their preferred learning styles.
7   To be successful, designers need to follow the principles already mentioned.
8   The same disciplines of meeting deadlines and responsiveness also need to apply in this virtual environment.

E-technologies have particular relevance in supporting virtual teams. This can involve you in being part of a global team or working with teams that are working virtually. Importantly, with virtual teams there is an even more pressing need to establish the ground rules for working together. This can include the following:

- identification of what technology support is available and how to make best use of it;
- agreement as to the frequency of meetings;
- commitment to attendance, on time and uninterrupted;
- agreement of team rules, e.g. responding to emails within a certain time-frame;
- ways of using time efficiently, e.g. defining the purpose of virtual meetings;
- using other methods to share information, e.g. circulating material prior to a meeting to allow everyone to come prepared to contribute;
- ideally from time to time physically getting together to form more substantial relationships;
- understanding each team member's expectations and needs when working virtually;
- constantly reassessing the opportunities for extending the technology support as systems improve, but using it appropriately,

e.g. not using valuable conference airtime on something that should have been emailed.

By remembering this checklist you have the opportunity to exploit the advantages and minimise the disadvantages of working virtually.

So how can blended learning support creativity?

As discussed, there are now numerous kinds of technology available, some of it very sophisticated and some more 'low-tech'. What is essential is that it is used effectively and imaginatively not just for creative young people but for all learners. The list is endless. In terms of access to multimedia, young people can create music, produce documentaries, create short films, photographic exhibitions or news-letters, create their own blogs, produce podcasts, learn web design, and use computer games to solve logic puzzles. Technology can also help the more reluctant learners. What this technology can do is allow creative ideas to be developed through a variety of media across all age groups. All it takes is access to the right equipment, supported by imaginative approaches from teachers who are excited and inspired by the new technology and who take children or students on a journey of creative discovery.

9 Creativity and employment

You can't shrink your way to greatness!

(Tom Peters)

Preparing young people for employment starts way before they reach school-leaving age; it even starts before conception. Their parents' and grandparents' hopes and aspirations, the community that they are born into and their country of birth all have an impact on the newborn's future. In Chapter 7 we talked about how 'Hope fires a neuron'. If a child is deprived of hope, their journey towards fulfilling their potential becomes that much tougher.

We have all heard the stories of hope overcoming adversity, but some children, for a variety of reasons, have a much tougher path to achieving their ideal career. Deprivation is not the only reason. For some children it is their well-meaning parents or teachers who stand in their way. There are many examples of adults who in mid-life turn to a completely different career, often with lower pay or prospects, or in a more radical environment, explaining that it was something they always wanted to do, but were persuaded away from it when they were younger and then found themselves unable to change career because of family commitments and responsibilities.

Careers advice

Careers advice in schools can unfortunately be less than effective, particularly for creative individuals. Businesses find it hard enough to manage their talent pools, but at least by that point a choice has been made. What career advice would you have given Leonardo da Vinci? Historically, parents, teachers and adults in general have told children to go for the safe option. In my grammar school there was a defined order. Girls were advised to undertake the following options:

- first choice: university;
- second choice: teacher training college;
- third choice: civil service;
- fourth choice: nursing;
- fifth choice: secretarial college.

Any deviation from this was frowned on and seen as a foolish strategy. Is today's advice any better, I wonder?

In *The Mismanagement of Talent* (2004), Brown and Hesketh suggest that 'There are new opportunities for people to use applied knowledge, initiative, and their creative energies in a wide range of occupations, including those working for small companies and self-employment.'

They quote Ghoshal and Bartlett (1997) (see 'Recommended reading'), who suggest that this requires a new approach to management. They argue that business leaders recognised:

> that human creativity and individual initiative were far more important as a source of competitive advantage than homogeneity and conformity . . . Their challenge was not to force employees to fit the corporate model of the 'Organization Man' but to build an organization flexible enough to exploit the idiosyncratic knowledge and unique skills of each individual employee.

Brown and Hesketh go on to highlight that the 'shift in focus from employment to employability reflects the view that many companies are no longer able (or willing) to offer long-term career opportunities to their managers, or professionals'. They state that this has led to the redefinition of the 'career' from a stepped progression within the same organisation over an extended career to that of a 'boundaryless' career. It recognises that 'the boundaryless career provides freedom and independence from . . . traditional organizational career arrangements'.

Employability reflects not only the new realities of business, but also changing lifestyles and cultural values. Brown and Hesketh argue that younger workers want jobs that offer excitement and new challenges that are difficult for any one organisation to provide. This has encouraged the creation of 'portfolio', 'boundaryless' or 'individual' careers that can include time out from the labour market to pursue other interests.

A trend that is being highlighted is a predicted increase in 'creative industries'. Richard Benson, writing in the *Guardian* (1 October 2005), quotes the Budget speech of Gordon Brown, Chancellor of the Exchequer, as saying that 'the creative industries were now bringing in 8% of the UK's national income and employing 1 in 20 of its workers'. He also said that Brown wanted to make 'Britain the "creative" workshop of the world'. Benson goes on to say that 'local governments see creative industries as engines for regeneration and businesses speak of creativity as a "core value" among school leavers'. Within the same article Benson talks about a growth in homeworking, with 'production being outsourced to individuals designing, writing and coding from a corner of their loft, shed, or kitchen table'.

If the above views are taken into consideration, it seems likely that schools are preparing young people for a world of work with the following attributes:

- greater access to university education by the masses;
- more competition for traditional roles;
- growth in portfolio careers;
- likelihood of several career changes;
- growth of the 'knowledge worker';
- potential of global working opportunities;
- growth of self-employment;
- the need to be enterprising both in corporate environments and in people's own businesses.

One of the challenges for creative people is selecting the right employment. Carol Eikleberry gives some very valuable advice in her book *The Career Guide for Creative and Unconventional People* (1999). Creative people, she suggests, 'want to do their own thing in their own way . . . Creative people are happier at work, and probably perform better, if they are given their freedom. They value autonomy.'

She suggests that:

> A sensitive intuitive expressive nature is no advantage when the task is to handle everyday maintenance chores by established rules. In fact, you may find that you are less efficient and more tired by the work than other people would be. Because so many of the jobs that are available are conventional jobs, you may get down on yourself and think, 'I just don't like to work.' You may not realize that it's just that particular kind of work not *all* work.

This equally can apply to children's experiences of school. If their first experiences of a new school are unsettling, it is likely that they will issue statements about not liking school and will shut down on the experience in total, instead of recognising that it might be one particular approach to teaching. Different people's experience of subject teaching often means that they believe they are 'bad' at a particular subject when in fact it may have been a result of the way that they were taught. This in part explains why some young people find more success in remedial classes; they have one-to-one teaching, the teachers appear more empathetic and they feel more able to ask questions about concepts that they don't understand.

Eikleberry claims that, when you do find work that fits your skills, you feel less stress. She quotes Bernard Haldene and 'dependable strengths', which he suggests come naturally to people: 'When you work with your natural strengths, you usually enjoy the process and feel you're doing it well. It's like flying with the wind, instead of against it.'

Helping young people recognise and acknowledge their skills, strengths and abilities is a critical part in helping them to prepare for the world of work. This has even more relevance with people who are creative. When they acquire this level of self-knowledge, they will be much better prepared for job hunting.

One way of doing this, Eikleberry suggests, is undertaking a skills analysis such as that contained within one of the most well-known career guides, *What Color Is Your Parachute?* (Bolles, 2006) (see 'Recommended reading').

She also suggests four questions to ask as a way of guiding career choices. It is potentially more effective with adults who will have had more experience, but it can be adapted for use with young people. The four questions should taken together, and supported with brainstorming the answers, as well as looking for linkages and connections between the answers:

1 'What are you doing when you are so engrossed or absorbed that you lose track of time?' Brainstorm; look for themes and patterns. Are there any trends?

2 'In what kinds of activities, relative to yourself and not others, do you make the boldest choices and take the greatest risks?' She suggests that it is very likely to be in those areas that you have the most intuitive confidence in yourself. Brainstorm; write the answers down. Do not restrict yourself to school or work; think about hobbies and extra-curricular activities.

3 'What are your occupational daydreams? Think about all work-related dreams, even as a child.' Many adults harbour unfulfilled dreams from childhood that parents or teachers steered them away from following. If using this with young people, the response will be more limited, but nonetheless will have a value, as it may open up their hopes and dreams.

4 'Another question is to consider how quickly you do certain tasks. Think of your skills in terms of running a race; anyone can cover the distance eventually, but the winner does it the quickest. Those areas where you work the most quickly relative to others are likely to be areas where you are most skilled.' Again this is a question that adults may find easier to answer, but you could extend it to homework or work outside school, for example. It is also about confidence: in which parts of the curriculum do they have most confidence with their answers?

What you are seeking to do with the responses is to encourage young people to start a process of identifying choices and options. It is not about defining a specific job; it is much more about creating self-awareness. It is also about exploring 'in the round'. As highlighted above, future generations will have a very different career path to that of their teachers. The concept of portfolio careers and the uncertainty about patterns of work mean that young people need the very strongest self-belief. All students will need to be able to apply creativity to their work patterns. There may also be times when they withdraw from the working environment. The creative person may do this from choice; for others it may be enforced by their employers; therefore all students need to develop resilience, which will sustain them through the bad times as well as the good.

In terms of making career choices, the challenge for creative people is often one of focus. They often find it hard to concentrate and, in terms of careers, may prefer to drift. There is some evidence that this is the reason why they extend their academic studies, as it gives them longer to put off decision making about a career. Equally, for others there is a challenge in that they believe that they are capable of many roles, and they are probably right, so making a choice can be difficult. One way through this is to ask them to identify what they definitely do not want to do.

'I definitely do not want to . . .' is quite an emotive statement but may reveal more valuable information than a response to 'What would you like to do?' However, from the 'don't want to' information there is an opportunity to start identifying what they may want in a future career.

At the beginning of a creative career individuals may not know what they are going to do or how to proceed. The most important action you can take to help them is to encourage them to accept their talents and to encourage them to explore the widest opportunities to use them. This is where school-to-work partnerships can help; unfortunately, work experience is not always a success. The need to identify a range of employers who are prepared to take responsibility for a young person for a short period of time can be a challenge. For some creative opportunities, it may be more difficult to encourage a creative worker to take responsibility for a young person (they often find it hard enough to organise their own lives, let alone be responsible for someone else!). In this context, one-off visits may be a better compromise. Whatever the opportunity there are a number of critical questions that should be asked:

- What do we know about the individual student's aspirations?
- Has this young person been given advice early enough to ensure

that their choice of study and qualifications match their likely career choice?

- How have we prepared both the student and the placement for the work experience?
- Have we encouraged the placement to share information about its overall 'employer brand', including vision, values, ethos, etc. (Thorne, *Employer Branding*, 2004 – see 'Recommended reading')?
- Will the placement experience match the student's choice of study or qualifications, and future career aspirations?
- How will the placement be structured? What opportunities will be available for the student to really gain valuable experience?
- How well briefed is the student about the world of work in general?
- Is there a preparation and debrief plan for the student and the placement?
- Is the student encouraged to use a variety of media to record the experience? (This will need to be checked with the placement, and advice given about recording with a camera or video.) The illustrated journal approach highlighted in Chapter 4 could be used to record the experience.
- How could you encourage the student to review, reflect on and maximise the learning experience, including sharing it with other students to build up all their portfolios of experience?

Another challenge for creative people is recognising that, for every person who welcomes their unusual take on the world, there will be many others who see them as disruptive, critical, challenging, dominant and self-centred. In addition, creative people often find prolonged recruitment processes frustrating. Given that they often find it difficult to select an occupation in the first place, once they have made up their mind they will just want to get started. Being rejected for a role is likely to have more impact on creative people than on others. Equally they may find it difficult to be contained within one role as they often feel that they can contribute across a wider spectrum.

Supporting a young person in making career choices

Planning the journey

One of the first stages in working with a student is to help them to identify what they really want to achieve. There can be a number of contexts for this; it is important to help them work through the key stages. For some students this may prove to be difficult if they have never had the opportunity to sit and review their hopes and dreams. Within a working environment, objective and goal setting tends to be work-related, e.g. 'What are you going to do to develop competence in the areas that this organisation needs?' In the context of school it's a combination of what they want to do in the short term and their longer-term aspirations; it will be partly about work, but also about their greater hopes and dreams. This will link closely with the vision and values of the 'brand Me' exercise on pages 124–8. You can also use the visualisation exercise from Chapter 4 to support this.

It will also be important to help them test reality. In today's working environment more than ever before, individuals have to cope with and handle change. It is essential that you help your learner to really explore their options and not to make assumptions based on what has happened to family and friends. This may include helping them to see the potential of lateral moves rather than assuming just one career.

You may also work with individuals who know what they want to do and have a very clear focus on the future. You may, however, be working with students who are suffering from a lack of confidence or self-esteem because of the feedback they have received from others in the past. Helping them to change their perspective may prove to be more of a challenge, because they may see the daily actions of others reinforcing this view, but some of the activities suggested in Chapters 4, 5 and 7 may help in this context.

Other students may find as a result of this exercise that what they thought they always wanted to do now no longer appeals. This may be because of a work placement or just because they are maturing and beginning to think seriously about their future. Importantly, they may need support to identify how they are going to develop the new skills or knowledge that they need. Again, think laterally. What other support could be available to them through night school, open learning or other routes?

Skills and knowledge audit

As well as the obvious measures such as examination results, increasingly young people are getting much wider exposure to the world of work through a variety of opportunities, including entrepreneurial school projects; therefore helping them to identify their skills and knowledge may also lead them to identify real areas of competence that they have developed. Encourage them to be confident, to really believe in their talents.

What would you like to do in the future?

Help them to consider answers to some of the questions below:

- What style and pattern of working?
- What responsibilities?
- What sectors attract you?
- What specific roles?
- What companies?
- What about location?
- What skills, competencies, training or new learning do you need?

What are my work-related goals?

- In three months' time I would like to have . . .
- In six months' time I would like to have . . .
- In 12 months' time I would like to have . . .
- What is it realistic to achieve in the short term?
- How could I break this down into bite-sized achievable goals?
- Who will offer me support?
- How will I measure my success?

What would I like to achieve out of work?

It is all too easy to focus on work-related goals, but particularly for young people it is important to encourage the broadest focus on their future. What are their hopes and aspirations? What are their ambitions?

Setting stretch goals

Goal setting should be undertaken in a context of the short, medium and longer term. Again, help the individual to succeed by encouraging them to set small targets that are achievable, as well as more aspirational and long-term goals. Use techniques such as SMART to help them identify the specifics. You may also need to have some examples to help them build their own set. By asking open questions, you can help the individual begin to identify areas that they wish to work on.

Be wary of asking an open question such as 'What do you want to do when you leave school?', as they simply may not know. It can be more helpful to start with broader objectives based on some skill development.

One other factor is to do with individual motivation. Usually what makes a significant difference in the achievement of goals is that the individual really wants to do it. Despite offering support to all students, you may find that some young people, faced with pressure on all sides to make a decision about their future, withdraw into themselves, and their real desire may not come until they have left school.

However, many young people are enthusiastic about their future and, based on the activity just discussed and using Figure 9.1, it will be possible to help them to create their own personal brand.

Creating the brand Me

Increasingly in today's business journals there is reference to personal branding, or brand Me. Tom Peters was one of the first advocates and, in a *Fast Company* article in 1997, 'The Brand Called You' (see 'Recommended reading'), he talks about becoming the 'CEO of Me Inc.':

> Regardless of age, regardless of position, regardless of the business we happen to be in, all of us need to understand the importance of

Figure 9.1 Brand Me © The Inspiration Network

branding. We are CEOs of our own companies: Me Inc. To be in business today, our most important job is to be head marketer for the brand called You.

Among other aspects he highlights the importance of visibility:

When you are promoting brand You, everything you do . . . and everything you choose not to do . . . communicates the value and character of the brand. Everything from the way you handle phone conversations to the emails you send . . . is part of the larger message you are sending about your brand.

In this context understanding the brand Me is going to be crucial for young people. In an environment driven by personal supply, being able to position yourself effectively will be vital. There is, however, a delicate balance between being personable and being 'in your face' and brash. This is where some of the personal branding work flounders. Just as some individuals feel uncomfortable with some of the image consulting advice, they will feel uncomfortable with personal branding. Done well, however, it can be invaluable to help young people gain a deeper understanding of themselves. From the key stages of Figure 9.1, here are some areas of focus.

What are my vision and values?

As in any marketing exercise, vision is one of the hardest areas to define, but it must be a real statement that the individual can identify with and, when asked, the student should clearly understand what they stand for. Interestingly, when schools run elections this is one of the rare times when individuals have to put together their vision and values as part of their manifesto. Research is showing that adults are now looking for alignment between their values and those of their employer organisation.

> When people truly share a vision they are connected, bound together by a common aspiration.
>
> (Peter Senge, *The Fifth Discipline*, 1990)

What are my personal traits and behaviours?

This is a key area where students need to gain a real understanding of how they appear to others. This is what we demonstrate daily in the way we interact with others, the way we conduct ourselves and the way we show our personal traits. It is also the area where we are at our most vulnerable. Often individuals get caught in patterns of behaving which are reinforced by the people and situations around them. Encouraging them to take the important first step is an essential part of the role of being a teaching coach. As with any comparable form of sports or ambition coaching, it is about encouraging the individual to move forward by focusing on self-belief and taking the first tentative steps forward. Giving helpful and constructive feedback on their behaviour can be valuable to young people, but, as we highlighted in Chapter 5, it needs to be focused on things that can be changed, and given in the context of a positive start and finish.

What are my skills and competences?

Encourage the student to identify what they can do. Help them to recognise what they are good at and to identify their strengths, and provide the opportunity for them to develop those skills. As already highlighted, it is important that clear objectives are set and regularly monitored and that an individual receives feedback and also has the opportunity to discuss their own view of their progress. In a coaching environment this will happen more naturally. Create opportunities to regularly recognise achievements, both individually and in the whole class.

What is different about me?

In marketing this would be defined as a USP, a unique selling proposition. What is my greatest strength? In a society where normal can equal bland, it is sometimes hard to encourage young people to identify where they feel that they are unique, but in an interview situation it can be their uniqueness that makes the difference in terms of them gaining a role. Equally, it may be their uniqueness which prevents them gaining a role. Unconventional and very creative people may need help in recognising that they may not succeed in gaining conventional roles if the recruiting organisation does not feel that it can accommodate them. As Gregory (2006) and Eikleberry (1999) both illustrate in their books (see 'Recommended reading'), people make choices about whether to conform or not, and some young people may decide that they do not want to conform to organisational norms. If this is the case they may need support in recognising the value of their uniqueness, which may also need to be identified and quantified in other ways, if for example they need to raise a bank loan to support the growth of their own business.

What is my essence?

'Essence', again a marketing term, is seen as the essential core of a product. What are the one or two sentences that sum me up? If someone was describing me to someone else, how would they describe me? What am I about? It is also about perception. How can I project my core essence to someone else? For example, 'I am a 16-year-old school leaver who . . .', 'I am a graduate who . . .' or 'I am X and I . . .'.

(The author has a number of profiles that will help both teachers and students identify individual preferences linked to creativity, innovation and Motivation to Change. For further details, email contact@theinspirationnetwork.co.uk)

What are the motivations for young people seeking work?

Something that is on the agenda of most companies is attraction and retention of talent; one of the most comprehensive and well-respected summaries of the key issues around talent is contained in *The War for Talent* (2001) by McKinsey & Company consultants Ed Michaels, Helen Handfield Jones and Beth Axelrod.

In a 1998 *Fast Company* article 'The War for Talent', Charles Fishman interviewed Ed Michaels, a McKinsey director who helped manage the original McKinsey study. There were a number of very interesting points made. The first was about access to talented people. Research in the US has shown that large companies are competing with start-ups for talent. The reason behind this is that people have the potential to make a lot of money, which was certainly the belief behind the original dot.com companies. Perhaps more importantly, they get the opportunity to be connected to the very top of the company at an earlier age, which has certainly been demonstrated in a number of successful young companies in both the UK and elsewhere.

In the interview Fishman asked Michaels 'What weapons can larger, more established companies use against start-ups and small companies?' Michaels suggested that the best weapons that large companies could use would be to mimic small companies and create smaller, more autonomous units. They could use their wealth to create more opportunity, but what they had to recognise was what motivated talented people. Perhaps the most significant part of the article was the identification of the best kinds of recruitment campaigns to attract talent, which gives an indication of where young people may be targeting their applications.

Michaels suggests that there are four kinds of messages:

- *Go with a winner.* This is for people who want a high-performing company where they're going to get lots of advancement opportunities.
- *Big risk, big reward.* The people who respond to this want an environment where they're challenged either to do exceptionally well or to leave – where there's considerable risk but good compensation, and where they can advance their career rapidly.
- *Save the world.* It attracts people who want a company with an inspiring mission and an exciting challenge – a pharmaceuticals or a high-tech company, for instance.
- *Lifestyles.* This is for people who seek companies that offer them more flexibility and better lifestyle benefits, such as a good location.

As I have mentioned in other chapters, some creative young people may find it challenging to fulfil their potential, particularly in a corporate environment, so it could be a very valuable exercise to use the above categories with young people to help them to identify what type of company they would identify with, and to identify some of the questions that they should be asking of future employers.

Networking

Connectivity was mentioned in the Introduction, and for all young people it is essential that they understand both the power and the importance of networking. It can sometimes get a bad press, but the ability to see the connections between people, the connections between ideas and the opportunities to link ideas and people to grow your network is an invaluable life skill. This is covered more in Chapter 11.

Enterprise and entrepreneurship

The success of television programmes like *The Apprentice* and *Dragon's Den* have fuelled even more interest from young people about setting themselves up in business. There are excellent schemes to encourage young people to try out their business skills. Some universities are now running enterprise, entrepreneurship or small business management as part of their business studies degrees. Durham University has a Centre for Entrepreneurship. Bournemouth University, recognising the growth in entrepreneurship, offers modules 'Starting a Business' and 'Entrepreneurship, Creativity and Innovation' as part of its business studies degree. The Arts Institute, also in Bournemouth, has an excellent Enterprise Pavilion containing incubation units for graduates, which has been very successful. (Contact details are given in Chapter 12.)

The Enterprise Pavilion (eP) is a new business centre for the creative industries. Joint-funded by the South West Regional Development Agency and the Arts Institute, the eP aims to support the growth of the creative industries in the region and increase graduate retention. It enables graduates in the creative industries to benefit economically from their knowledge by giving them advice, resources and support to set up and run their own businesses. As part of this package, the eP offers affordable and flexible high-quality office or studio accommodation on an easy-in, easy-out basis.

Schools too are providing students with increasing opportunities to run small businesses. An excellent example is Writhlington School, a business and enterprise specialist school that has achieved widespread recognition for its ambitious Orchid Project, not just for high-quality growing techniques, but for the way it has adapted this project to focus on enterprise and conservation. As well as establishing links with the Royal Botanic Gardens at Kew, it is also working with the Eden Project in Cornwall to supply seedlings to the tropical biome. In May 2006, the Orchid Project won a coveted gold medal in the category of 'lifelong learning' at the RHS Chelsea Flower Show.

What is also important is having enterprising teachers with the dedication, commitment and drive to make these projects work. One Writhlington student was interviewed on television about his involvement in the project. His initial expectation had been that it would be a fairly typical school greenhouse project growing a few seedlings; he had no idea about the scale, scope and success of the project. Helping young people to have faith in their ideas, to think beyond their immediate environment and to be enterprising supports their acquisition of crucial life skills.

One of the biggest challenges for creative young people will be application and focus. Just having the great ideas will not be enough. Anyone who wants to bring an idea to market has to progress beyond the 'aha' moment. Identifying how they prefer to work is another critical part of their decision-making process.

Some enterprising people work together more as independent partners, each committed to their own particular role, with the achievement of the spirit of enterprise based on a cooperative approach.

The workplace of today is one where only those who take control of their own destiny survive. The survivors will be those people who learn to act in an enterprising manner in every aspect of their lives. They will no longer rely upon someone else to plan and develop their careers, identify and schedule their work, set goals, review their performance and source new opportunities.

Everyone can work in an enterprising manner; it's just a question of unlearning old habits and replacing them with new ones. The place, pace and nature of work are changing rapidly, and it is becoming more a case of the possession and use of knowledge than the application of physical skill.

Being enterprising is about:

* being intrigued by new concepts;
* identifying opportunities to develop new business;
* creating new and innovative ways of developing an existing idea;
* developing new ideas, processes or products;
* being able to takes calculated risks;
* offering independent ideas;
* challenging the status quo;
* turning creative ideas into an effective business solution;
* having personal energy and reliance to keep going when the going gets tough.

Creative young people may very well be interested in being self-employed or working for a small business, but it is important that they realise that the enterprise option is not a 'soft choice'. Most entrepreneurs work incredibly hard, particularly in the early set-up years. Below is a set of questions to help them start to explore the option.

The enterprise top 20 questions

1   Do I know the value of what I can offer? Could I put a price on it?
2   How resourceful am I?
3   Does the thought of being more in control of my own destiny excite me?
4   How good am I at sticking with an idea? Am I resilient?
5   Do I adopt a 'Just do it!' principle?
6   How far do I look ahead when considering the possible impact of business decisions?
7   What actions do I take to think laterally and strategically?
8   How creative am I? What actions do I take to generate new ideas?
9   Do I come up with unconventional solutions to ongoing problems?
10 How easy is it for me to spot connections and linkages between apparently unrelated factors?
11 Do I think around a problem?
12 Can I spot new trends?
13 How good am I at building on existing new ideas? Am I an early adopter?
14 Am I prepared to champion a good idea?
15 Do I put new ideas through rigorous testing?
16 Do I learn from mistakes?
17 Can I convince others of the value of doing things differently?
18 Do I allow myself time to consider all the issues, explore all possibilities and consult with others when making key business decisions? How often do I discuss issues with others with a different viewpoint to help me find a solution?
19 Am I prepared to learn very different ways of working?

20 Do I have a good network? How many business contacts do I have? Who do I know who could help me?

Finally, in response to the questions above, if I know the answers to all of this, what is stopping me? Why don't I just do it?

Through the unknown, we'll find the new.

(Charles Baudelaire)

10 Fulfilling your creative potential

Faced with a pile of marking, Monday morning, an unruly class, difficult parents, demanding school head, unhelpful colleagues and challenging governors, you could easily forget that there is a creative world waiting to be discovered.

How well do you know yourself? How far do you push the boundaries of discovery? What do you do to inspire yourself? Would you describe yourself as creative? Over the years I have worked with many people in helping them develop their creativity. What is interesting is how many people are reluctant to acknowledge their creativity. If I ask a group of any age 'Would you describe yourself as creative?', there is a lot of looking down at their hands. Very few people want to acknowledge that they might be creative. I have also heard very young children say, 'I cannot draw. I'm rubbish at art.' What is important in any debate about creativity is to recognise the scale and scope of it. It is not just about the arts; it has a much broader perspective than that. If we take the dictionary definition from Chapter 2, 'Inventive and imaginative, creating, or able to create' (*Concise Oxford Dictionary*, 9th edition), it is possible to see that this can be applied to any discipline. I would also venture to suggest that it is almost impossible to be a teacher if you do not have some element of creativity. I know that some teachers feel that some of the constraints of the curriculum are denying them their creativity, but most respond with energy and vigour to accommodate the curriculum within their creative mindsets. In some cases the ingenuity of their ideas and the opportunities that they create for learning go much further than the standards suggested in the National Curriculum.

Where these ideas come from is sometimes hard to define. Inspiration cannot easily be anchored down and looked at. It is a sense, a feeling and a mood, something that lifts you above the ordinary and enables you to achieve something special. Being inspired transcends the normal day-to-day activities. I have already mentioned 'flow', and more and more people are becoming aware of how this works. There are techniques that stimulate it which have already been mentioned. It is, however, I think, worth mentioning again that there are conditions that help to stimulate creativity.

'What are the best conditions that help you to be creative or innovative?'

This was one of the questions in a survey that I asked for *Managing the Mavericks* (Thorne, 2003 – see 'Recommended reading').

The responses reveal a richness of stimuli, ranging across outside environments to organisational teams and individuals' own domestic space. A number of respondents gave examples of when they are in 'flow'. Freedom is often mentioned, as is feeling relaxed and, when discussing preferred working environments, a need to be stimulated through the senses. Other people are also important for some respondents, either as sounding boards or just to talk to, socialise with or have there to welcome them back from their thinking time. Others mention that deadlines, challenges and pressure also help them to be creative.

Their sources of inspiration were equally varied:

> Anything new, a place I haven't seen before, a picture on a card or post card, a quote I haven't heard before, lyrics in songs, videos, stories in books or magazine articles, driving with nothing on my mind and suddenly a thought comes in that is somehow everything I have been waiting for but didn't know it.

> Events, other people, but mostly 'voices' in my head!

> Books, pictures, images, songs, landscapes, memories, connections, others.

> Thinking time and believing anything is possible.

Aesthetics, nature, music, people.

Being in water, in the bath, or swimming, ideally in an empty swimming pool with a notepad nearby to capture the thoughts.

Inspirational moments in life. This may either be something in nature, music, something I've read, an actual event. I think this mainly relates to situations in which I see the hidden strength, the focus of conviction, beating the odds, excelling, all these types of things.

Identifying sources of inspiration

As has been highlighted throughout this book we are all different and as such will be inspired in very different ways, but here are some thoughts to add to those above. One way of being inspired is to start looking much more closely at the things around you.

The French Impressionists were a group of painters who tried to change the traditional French approach to art by reproducing visual impressions rather than painting something as it would normally look. They tried to capture a moment in time, sometimes painting scenes over and over again because of the impact of light at different times of the day. They went out into fields and by rivers, stood in front of mountains and just painted what they saw. Often we rush around from one task to the next, barely stopping. One way of stimulating your creativity is to take a camera and go and take some pictures, not just happy snaps but photographs with meaning, including close-ups and unusual angles. Look at the textures on a wall, patterns, cloud formations, industrial landscapes, pastoral scenes, seascapes, rooftops and sporting subjects. Go down low and look up high. Imagine you are entering a competition for the most unusual picture. Photography can be absorbing and can help you to observe in a different way.

Go to an art gallery and go as close to a painting as a curator will let you; marvel at the detail in the brush strokes; now back right away. What is different? Visit modern art and some old masters; look at sculptures; try to get inside the artist's mind. Look at some more obscure art; see if you can identify what the artist is trying to say.

When people's lives are busy they sometimes forget what richness exists simply by observing, and consequently their creativity doesn't flow because it cannot fight its way through the clutter.

Another way of stimulating your creativity is to practise being an artisan. Traditionally, artisans are workers and craftspeople; they create things; they make bread, grow vegetables and carve in wood or stone. In today's society, many people have a secret dream of being an artisan, creating things to sell at a local market. While this may seem a romantic dream, the making of things is another way to slow down and let your creativity flow. While kneading the bread or tending plants you may suddenly find you have thought of the solution to a problem that has been bothering you for weeks.

You may feel that you lack the skills to do anything creative, but most things can be taught. It's never too late to learn a musical instrument, to take singing or dancing lessons, or to learn to paint or sculpt. You may not become a Michelangelo or a Renoir, but you can have tremendous fun learning, and what you create will give you as much a sense of achievement as if it were a masterpiece. This doesn't apply just to making things. Designing a garden, instructing an architect or finding a solution to a problem can all involve creativity.

Some people have always wanted to write – poetry, novels, short stories. Julia Cameron in *The Artist's Way* (1995) suggests writing three pages of writing every morning. What she suggests these three pages do is allow you to get past your belief that you cannot write or that you are not creative; they allow you to get past your 'Censor'. She suggests that 'Logic Brain is our Censor', but:

> Artist Brain is our creative holistic brain. It thinks in patterns and shadings. It sees a fall forest and thinks: Wow! Leaf bouquet! Pretty! Gold-shimmery-earthskin-king's carpet. Artist's brain is associative and free-wheeling. It makes new connections, yoking together images to invoke meaning, like the Norse myths calling a boat a 'wave-horse'. In *Star Wars* the name Skywalker is a lovely artist-brain flash.

Danny Gregory takes a similar view in *The Creative License* (2006) when he suggests that, when drawing a mug, initially your left brain will tell you 'You can't draw' or 'This is too hard.' At some point, he suggests, your left brain will get bored and wander off, thus releasing your right brain, which 'has much less of a sense of time, or rules, or rigidity and will take you to a relaxed alpha state'.

This is a principle that can be applied to anything; the toughest part is starting, allowing yourself the luxury of doing something creative just for you.

Idea generation

So where do people get their ideas from? In reality there are a number of sources and triggers, and the more you open your mind up to learning and use different approaches and techniques the easier you will find it to identify new ideas.

If you want to stimulate your mind to come up with ideas, the secret is to relax and let your subconscious do the work. Ideas often occur when we are least expecting them and when we are doing other things. Many people who have been searching for a solution to a problem find the solution occurs once they go and do something else. As already mentioned, this can happen when you are doing something quite mundane like cleaning the car, ironing or taking part in some physical activity.

However, what is even more important is that, when your mind is clear and your ideas are running freely, you need to make the most of this special time. If you find that you have hit a creative period, you need to capture your thoughts because they will come at a pace which may surprise you. Some people find it easy to generate ideas, but most find it a challenge; therefore you need to use a variety of methods to help you stimulate your mind. When you find your creativity is being stifled, take a break and do something completely different. Take regular time out to indulge yourself. Use others for support and to bounce ideas off, however crazy. Build on initial fleeting thoughts to anchor more tangible concepts. Unlearn lessons from childhood; say 'I can' instead of 'I can't'.

One way of doing this is to ensure that you always have something nearby which will capture these moments. You can have a high-tech or low-tech approach to this, utilising small notepads, PDAs or small tape recorders. As mentioned in earlier chapters, some people keep journals almost as a catalogue of their best ideas. Others create mood boards or ambition walls.

Some people find that they need to create a special environment to be creative. This may be a special place, a desk or a room at home which becomes the focus for your thinking time. In this environment they may create special conditions where, as though preparing for an exam, they assemble fresh paper and sharpened pencils and shut themselves away from the rest of the family and work at their projects. Other people go running or take part in some other kind of physical activity.

These creative sessions can be very tiring, and you may have very high creative output followed by periods when you find it difficult to concentrate. The difficulty can be in trying to create the feeling of flow, rather than waiting for it to happen. You may be aware that you feel better at certain times of the day. If you do experience this sensation you will know if you are a morning person or a night owl. Those who have owl-like tendencies find that at night they have lots of energy. Just as everyone else is getting ready for bed they start waking up, sometimes wanting to go out. They feel hungry and find it difficult to go to sleep before midnight. The morning person, however, finds it difficult to lie in bed in the morning. They are usually awake early, but in the evening find it difficult to stay awake after 10.30.

Many of us, because of the nature of where we work, have spent years trying to adapt our body clock to meet the demands of the workplace. Understanding how your body responds can help you get the best out of different situations. There are a number of things that you can do to help your flow. Using your senses can have a tremendous effect on your creativity. Identifying images, pieces of music and sounds that help to inspire you can improve your ability to get started and to help you keep going.

Who do I know who inspires me?

In Chapter 11 the value of networking is highlighted, but there may be one or two people who you know have that special ability to inspire you. Treasure them and value what they can offer you and also see if you can inspire them too. Finding a soulmate is a very special feeling; never take the relationship for granted. You may want to try to find a creative coach, someone who really understands the creative process or who has a particular creative talent and will help you really develop your creativity.

I talked about being original in Chapter 6 and the importance of encouraging gifted children to maintain their originality. What is equally important is to recognise synchronous activity. When two or more people have similar thoughts it is often described as synchronicity, particularly if the people did not necessarily know each other beforehand. The more you explore your creativity, the more you open up and share your thoughts with others, the more likely it is that these synchronous events will happen. If you follow particular trains of thought you will identify writers and researchers who think like you do. When I shared the original full 'Mavericks Talking' research report with the respondents, many of them contacted me to say that they found it very difficult to identify their own response because they could have said almost anything in the report, so similar were the thoughts of others.

In terms of creativity, working with like-minded people can help you explore and take ideas further. We all have preferences in how we generate ideas. Some of us will prefer to be the person who generates the idea in the first place and, if you are one of these people, as I highlighted in Chapter 2 you may almost be plagued with good ideas. What can help you is to identify someone who can build on your ideas and take them on to the next level, but then it can be helpful to have someone who can begin to evaluate these ideas, to help you sift through what is realistic and achievable.

Once an idea has been tested then it can be helpful to have support from people who are able to help you either plan or implement the idea. Once it is being implemented then it is important to have someone who is able to measure the effectiveness of the idea and, where appropriate, share best practice with others. In this way a whole team of people with different preferences can work together on the implementation of an idea and play to their strengths.

Here are some ideas to help you stimulate your creativity:

• Take time to identify what really inspires you. Where do you go to stimulate your creativity? How often do you take time out just to think? What opportunities do you take outside of work to see, or take part in, creative activities? Try to visit art galleries, museums, theatres and concerts.

- Who do you know who thinks differently from you? What could you learn from them? How open is your mind? How often do you say 'Why don't we try this?' rather than 'We've tried it before; it won't work'?

- When did you last do something creative? Take opportunities to be creative: write, draw and take up creative hobbies. Explore the whole range of creative actions. What would you really like to do that is different?

- Share ideas with others; use 'displayed thinking', where ideas are incubated by a continuous process of brainstorming when the originators of the ideas allow others to add their input. Think creatively – do you have contacts in other parts of the world who could add to your knowledge?

- Practise lateral thinking; use some of the resources in Chapter 12; use different tools and techniques to help you think more creatively. Do not cling to the past; become an 'early adopter' of new ways of working. Be prepared to experiment with ways of working differently.

- Share your thoughts with colleagues with different styles of thinking; take time to explore how you can work together and how the process would work. Recognise that some people will have creativity in working within the curriculum while others will want to work more with the idea generation process. Play to people's strengths.

- Make connections with other schools and colleges. Think about how you could create imaginative projects for your students. How could your ideas link different parts of the curriculum? The incubation of genuinely new products or processes may not be easily achieved within the normal day-to-day constraints of the timetable or curriculum. Explore creative ways of developing a test-bed environment. Consider alternative methods of stimulating production.

- Assess the education marketplace. Who are the originators? Spot new trends and be prepared to analyse their potential application on behalf of your school. Who are the imitators? What are the advantages of being first to market? Do you have a commercial idea that could be taken to the education market? How could you apply what you have discovered within your school or the bigger education marketplace?

- When faced with a problem within your school, encourage your colleagues to think creatively around the problem. Use creativity techniques like brainstorming and SWOT (strengths, weaknesses, opportunities and threats). Strengths and weaknesses usually apply to current and internal factors, opportunities and threats to future and external influences. Come up with new ways of handling traditional problems.

- Develop a template of screening questions which will help present new ideas to the rest of your colleagues. What advantages will they bring for our students, for other schools and for education in general? Why has it not been done before? Not all ideas need to be new. Do not 'reinvent the wheel'; take time to recognise what already works well and find ways of developing this or find new ways of using existing ideas within your school. Follow ideas through carefully to the implementation stage, taking note of the progress and issues at each stage. Once implemented, regularly monitor their success.

- Make sure that ideas are not prematurely shut down. When ideas do not work out as planned, take the opportunity to review the reasons for the lack of success. Make a habit of asking 'How would I do it differently next time?' Invite and listen to ideas from students, who may challenge the status quo. Do not always give up on an idea if it hasn't worked the first time. Good ideas often fail to be adopted initially. With careful planning and analysis it is possible to re-present an idea more successfully on a second occasion.

- Be prepared to champion an idea that you passionately believe in. Work to maintain sponsorship throughout the life cycle of the idea.

- Identify colleagues with a different viewpoint whose opinion you trust to review your idea and to give you critical feedback. Keep putting your ideas through rigorous testing.

- Some people have difficulty in translating their vision into a strategy for implementation; find others who are capable of supporting you to move your idea from dream into reality. Identify people in your network who would be effective mentors, or sponsors of your ideas. Regularly meet with them to update them on progress and to use them as sounding boards.

A little bit of magic!

However well motivated you are there may be times when you need to recharge or to be inspired to go on to the next stage. This section is about getting that charge of electricity to help you on your journey towards reaching your creative potential.

Do you have special pieces of music which energise or relax you? Do you have a special photograph or picture which, when you look at it, invites you to become part of the scene? Do you have special places or people that you visit to help you recharge and become 'centred' (feeling at peace) again? Do you keep near you special quotes that inspire you? A number of people whom I have worked with have created their own personal books in which they collect thoughts about how they are feeling, their goals, pictures and quotes as records of the progress they are making. This is like the concept of illustrative journaling that was discussed in Chapter 4. As well as our own personal collection of special moments, there are techniques that we can use to help us.

Visualisation

Some people have what is called a 'photographic memory', a wonderful advantage in exams but even more useful in conjuring up visual memories with which to rejuvenate and energise themselves. Imagine being able to recall a scene from your photograph album in 3D colour and stereophonic sound every time you felt you were having a particularly tough day. We explored examples of this in practice in the classroom in Chapter 4, but it applies to self-motivation too.

Visualisation is a tool which we can all use to help us feed our subconscious with powerful visual images. We can seal into our minds positive images of times when we were successful or times of great joy and happiness or simply an image of a tropical beach with silver sand and impossibly blue waves stretching far into the distance.

We can train our minds to hear the sounds; we can feel the heat of the sun or the texture of the sand.

Make the best use of each day

Do you remember your own school assemblies? There was meant to be more meaning to them than just sitting wriggling on a cold wooden floor. The hope was that the readings and the hymns would inspire you to go back to your classroom ready to learn so that you would grow up and do great things. Do you start each day with a motivational thought? Do you actually make a positive affirmation, 'Today is going to be great!', as you get out of bed? At the end of the day, do you close it by sorting your outstanding issues into a pile and allowing your mind to solve the problems overnight?

Be a child

If you watch children playing, two thoughts usually occur. One is an amazement at how they can become completely absorbed in a task, particularly if it is tactile, involving paint, or sand, or building something. The second is the tremendous amount of energy they have; they are constantly on the go, rushing around, laughing and chasing each other, hiding, falling over, getting up and going again. When was the last time that you had that much energy?

Once in a while, indulge the child in you. Forget the responsibilities, be indulgent, do things that give you real pleasure, eat childlike foods, watch cartoons, do a jigsaw, build a castle or paint: forget the adult in you; be a child!

Think about the environment you live in

We may not all live where we want to live, but inside the four walls of your house, flat or even bedsit you can personalise it to reflect your own taste and imagination. Some people adopt the principles of feng shui, but, whether you are an advocate or not, there is much that you can do to create an environment that allows you to rest and switch off from the rest of the world. This is particularly important if you are working in tough teaching environments. Equally, you can invest in one or two pieces of furniture, or pictures, or pottery, that just inspire you because of their aesthetic quality. Having freshly ground coffee, a newspaper delivered or fresh flowers in the hall can lift a house into a home. There is an advertisement on the television about breakfast in New York. I can never watch it without almost smelling the waffles, seeing the bagels and wanting to drink the drink. There is a similar advertisement about the food department of a well-known UK store which also appeals to our senses. Does your home stimulate your senses?

Do something exciting, interesting or challenging with other people

Increasingly, people are living on their own and, although teachers are often quite sociable, meeting up out of school or college, there could be the opportunity to meet with different people, raise money for charity, take part in a project or fulfil an ambition. Gaining a different perspective on life, possibly living in a different country, going on a trek or taking an educational holiday abroad may be just the stimulus you need.

Research is showing that young people want more from life. What about their teachers?

Seize the moment!

If you struggle to be childlike, at least recognise the need to take a break and do the pleasurable things that you are normally too busy to do. Go through your diary and identify times when you know you can get away, plan them in and do everything you can to keep to them.

It is important to realise too that not every act of creativity involves vast planning and serious thought. It is very easy to go into an art shop and buy what you need to paint a picture, and even easier to buy a pen, pencils and a pad to draw on. At the other end of the scale, in today's global environment everything is much more accessible. If you are looking for inspiration, apart from visiting local museums or art galleries, a visit to the Guggenheim Museum in New York or Venice or lunch in Paris is now within the grasp of most people. It does, however, require an attitude of mind. It is that initial 'get up and go' philosophy that says 'Let's do something really different with the spare time in our lives.'

> There are no bad drawings. Drawings are experiences. The more you draw, the more experience you get ... Release your ego's desire for perfection. Take risks, grow, create as much as you can, whenever you can.
>
> (Danny Gregory, *The Creative License*, 2006)

11 Doing it differently
How to enrich your life

> Connecting with one's dreams releases one's passion, energy and excitement about life . . . The key is uncovering your ideal self – the person you would like to be, including what you want in your life and work . . . Developing that ideal image requires a reach deep inside to one's gut level.
>
> (Daniel Goleman *et al.*, *The New Leaders*, 2002)

If you are a teacher, coach or learning designer, you may spend almost all of your working life helping others to soar, but what about you? When was the last time that you thought about your own hopes, dreams and ambitions? When did you take time out to indulge in creative thinking or to enrich your senses?

If you want to learn how to soar, before you take off you need to draw on your innate wisdom about yourself and to really explore your potential to help you reach your greatest heights.

Have you achieved everything that you want to achieve in your life? Have you fulfilled all your potential? How do you feel today? How did you feel when you first awoke? Were you motivated, full of energy, racing to get up and get started on the day? Or did you turn the alarm off, pull the covers over your head and want to go back to sleep?

Very few of us are fortunate enough to wake up naturally each day full of positive thoughts. However, it is possible to find ways of focusing our energy into a more positive way of thinking. If you are constantly helping others, it is very easy to neglect yourself. If you are trying to be more creative or to help others, it is important to be able to recharge your batteries and to develop an inner resilience. This chapter is about you taking time out for you, but it will have a relevance in your work with others too. It also relates to many of the earlier chapters, for example in the context of the brand Me work discussed in Chapter 9. What is your personal brand?

How confident are you?

You may be one of those people mentioned in Chapter 5 in relation to the study carried out by Carnegie-Mellon University with several hundred 'knowledge workers':

> Superior performers intentionally seek out feedback, they *want* to hear how others perceive them, realising that this is valuable information. That may also be part of the reason people who are self-aware are better performers. Presumably their self-awareness helps them in a process of continuous improvement.

Knowing their strengths and weaknesses, and approaching their work accordingly, was a competence found in virtually every star performer. The authors of the study stated, 'Stars know themselves well.'

Alternatively, you may suffer from some of the self-doubts of respondents in the 'mavericks' research mentioned in Chapter 2: 'Getting others to see what's inside your head and appreciate it' or 'Never believing that I am done or that it is good enough'.

Many creative people suffer from self-doubt. Artists, writers, actors and presenters often talk about that moment of nervousness before they perform, exhibit or have a book published. While on the one hand it often gives them 'an edge' which makes them perform better, they still have to overcome it. How self-aware are you?

As the Goleman quote on page 147 states, however confident you may be, to really fulfil all your potential you may have to dig a little deeper. Going on your own personal journey of discovery can have real value when you are trying to help others fulfil their potential.

Corporate business conferences often start with inspirational music, or videos which display the company vision and values accompanied by strong images and music. Many coaches helping national teams prepare for internationals put together inspirational tape recordings and videos to help their teams focus on winning. What is increasingly being recognised is the importance of visualising the success and experiencing what success feels like.

Self-knowledge

To help you take ownership, here are some questions that you may want to ask yourself:

- *What do I really know about me?* How you describe yourself to others is only the very top layer. Underneath is a whole cocktail of hopes and fears, attitudes and behaviours. When you apply for a job you often are asked to complete a variety of tests which may give you information about your personality traits, skills and aptitudes. However, if you stay in the same role for many years you may not have the opportunity to gain as much self-knowledge. The more you know about you, the more you understand about how you will respond in certain situations. So take every opportunity presented to you to build up your picture of yourself. Try to observe other people and see how they react to different circumstances. If you are thinking about doing something different, take the opportunity to get mentally fit.
- *What do I do really well?* One of the failings in society at large is to give people enough positive feedback about what they have done well. We rarely thank people individually when they have done something for us. Equally, individuals often do not know how to respond when they are thanked or given a compliment; there is a lot of looking down and shuffling. Knowing what you do well and taking time to thank others are important parts of building confidence. Making a list of your strengths is an important first step in gaining self-knowledge.
- *What would I like to do better?* As well as knowing your strengths it is also important to recognise areas that you need to work on. By identifying them for yourself you can take responsibility for improving them. We all have things that we would like to improve, but there may also be areas where you say, 'Actually,

I don't think I will ever be able to do that well. Who do I know who I could work with to complement my skills and help me?' In terms of developing your creativity, what are the areas that really interest you? What would you enjoy doing? Is it just a case of practising more, or do you need tuition?

- *How do I react under pressure?* There is a maturity of approach which only comes by self-discovery. There is a big difference between handling stress and handling pressure. People can respond positively and actually withstand a certain amount of pressure, but the physical impact of stress can be quite different. You need to ask yourself what puts you under pressure and then find ways of coping with it. Getting yourself in shape physically and mentally can be an important part of your preparation to get more out of life.

- *What will prompt me into taking action?* One of the biggest reasons why people do not get the most out of their lives is that there is always a reason not to get started, to get deflected from your goals and to give up when it gets difficult. If you understand how to motivate yourself and make your goals more achievable, it suddenly becomes much easier to get started and to keep going.

- *What is really important in my life?* Before starting on the journey of self-discovery, it is often helpful to take stock and identify what is important to you, particularly if you really do want to do things differently. You need to anchor what you want to nurture and cherish and identify what is less important. Physically clearing out the clutter that surrounds you is another way of getting ready.

- *Who do I trust to give me feedback?* We all need feedback, as it helps us to grow and develop and to gain a greater understanding of our strengths and development areas, but we also need to find the right people to give it to us. Unfortunately, too few people are really skilled at giving it. Try to find people whose opinion you trust and value and ask them to help you understand yourself better.

The more insight you gain, the better able you are to self-motivate and to harness your energy and talents to achieve any of your ambitions, not just to increase your creativity. Many hopes and dreams never come to fruition because people make it too difficult for themselves to achieve them. The greater your self-knowledge, the more able you are to create the situations and to identify the support which will help you to achieve what you want most out of life.

So how do you put all this self-knowledge into practice?

The answer is that you can do it only through focus, by having a clear vision and values, and really recognising what you can achieve if you invest in your talents. Teaching is one of those professions where there tends to be job security; therefore it is very easy just to cruise through a career without fully exploring your potential. You may work incredibly hard, but you may also hide your talents, not recognising what else you could do and what you could share with others.

You are the most important person in achieving your full potential. It is so easy to accept what we have achieved and just to give up on ambitions. You can be so busy developing others that you forget to develop yourself. Others can help you, but ultimately it is your strength of will-power which will make the difference between you drifting through life and achieving your full potential. Many people feel that they could be brilliant if only someone gave them the chance. Hard as it may seem, we often have to take that important first step ourselves.

Believe in yourself!

Picture the scene: you hit upon an idea, it's off-the-wall and different, but it involves an element of risk. Something inside you tells you it could work. Your partner, friends, family or work colleagues, however, caution you by saying it won't work or it's too risky. What do you do? You have no evidence of its potential other than a gut feel that it is worth trying. Many people hesitate, particularly if they are close to their partner, friends or family and respect their judgement, and perhaps a little voice inside you says they may be right. You resist the idea, channel your energies elsewhere, and then six months or a year later someone else is successful with your idea. How do you feel then?

Most brilliant business ideas are very simple, often based initially on someone taking a chance. This book isn't about encouraging you to take foolish, outrageous risks but more about moving beyond the 'what ifs' and on some occasions taking a calculated risk or step into the unknown. The reason why we have to take risks is that sometimes we are moving into the unknown. The great explorers, inventors and scientists had to do exactly that because often no one had been there before them.

Many ordinary people's ambitions are based on doing what they have seen someone else do successfully. Therefore we have role models or case studies. In most cases, someone will have been there before and you can learn from their experience. Apart from learning from others, it is still essential to have that inner belief, a desire to achieve or a driving force which will help you to rise above people or situations that appear to be trying to hold you back.

Networking

Another important source of support is a network; the best networks are built up over years by valuing other people, being genuinely interested in them and just being very natural. It is very easy to build up a network, but you need to keep nurturing it. Some people are absolutely brilliant at networking and consequently are often able to find solutions by talking to people whom they know. It is never too late to start, and once started it is much easier to keep going. So how do you start?

First, think about whom you could put on your map of contacts. Always think beyond the obvious. As well as close family, friends and the people you work with, think about people you know from your own past, people you went to school with or those from previous employment. What about those who offer you a professional service, like your bank manager, solicitor, dentist or members of the leisure centre?

Do you make contact with the parents of your children's friends? What about your partner's work colleagues and their partners? Do you belong to any professional associations?

If you are not naturally comfortable with the concept of net-working, start in a way which is comfortable for you. Networking is not just a one-way process; people will equally want you in their network. It is all part of the philosophy of helping others. Effective networking requires a lightness of touch which is based on helping each other and sharing good fortune.

People who are skilled at networking have a network of people who vary between those who are very close and those whom they have less contact with but whom they can call upon for help if required. The best networks are the ones that are reciprocal and where it is fun to be a member.

Achieving a balance

One of the most frequent concerns of people trying to do things differently with their life is time. Despite advances in technology, most people today are working harder than ever. Most organisations, including schools, have fewer people doing more work. Extended hours, marking and after-school activities all add up to additional time. In the majority of families the two adults work; consequently the demands on 'free time' are enormous. Congested roads, patterns of travel and longer working hours often mean that people are spending their most productive and creative time at work, only to arrive home believing that they are too tired to do anything other than watch the television and go to bed. This cycle can repeat itself for months or years.

Alternatively, you can take control and say that work has so many hours of your time and during that time it will get the best from you. At certain other times of the day, however, you are going to take a break and that time will be for you. Many people work through their lunch breaks, just grabbing a sandwich. Within the constraints of school commitment and timetabling, would the world fall apart if they got up and went out for 30 minutes? The answer is probably not, but the response is usually 'If I took a break in the middle of the day people would think I was taking advantage or shirking' or 'How can I go out when my colleagues are working so hard?' In reality, the solution depends on your agreed terms and conditions and also the prevailing local culture.

Some people prefer to arrive early and to take short, or no, lunch breaks so that they can go home early. Sometimes this is because of family commitments or simply because they want to be away from work. However, if you then arrive home really tired from having worked too long with no breaks you may want to consider other arrangements. It is now well recognised that the right exercise and eating the right foods are an important source of energy. Therefore you may wish to analyse how your life is currently organised and plan in some time for exercise and thinking.

Organisations are still slow to recognise the need for reflective times for creative thinking. The difficulty is keeping time for yourself instead of devoting it to other people. Most people have additional demands to those of the workplace. Partners, children, parents, the home, the garden and the car all need care and attention. Spend a moment and list the demands on your time, add that to the amount of time you spend at work, eating and sleeping, subtract that from 24 hours and multiply by 7 to give you the amount of time you have available each week to try to do things differently.

Many of you may have arrived at minus figures. If this is the case you may need to prioritise and reschedule your time. Many time management books talk about finding an extra hour or a 'magic hour'. The way that this is achieved is to look at your normal use of time and to reschedule or switch priorities.

Although at first this may seem an impossible task, if you want to do something enough you will do it. Many people who want to achieve something different squeeze extra time out of already full days. The same applies to swimmers, rowers, runners, skaters and sportsmen and women worldwide, all of whom take part in gruelling training sessions when many of the rest of us are asleep. This raises the question of how much sleep you really need and why it is important for you to really get to know your body; then you know how to plan to keep it regularly charged with energy.

Taking ownership

Many people have to overcome past prejudices and feelings before they can start working towards ambition, for example:

- 'I don't deserve it.'
- 'I'm not good enough.'

- 'I need to work hard before . . .'
- 'What about the risks?'
- 'Can I really do it?'

What stops them is unhelpful people fuelling their doubts. Do you think you really can? Should we take the risk? What if something happened to you, me and us?

Overcoming objections

The question when handling objections is to identify where the objections are coming from and why. Some of the objections may be your own. You may find yourself feeling almost schizophrenic when you argue with yourself about when to start or whether to go for the ambition at all. In the case of other people it is important to identify the root of the objection or why they don't want you to do something.

Much of it is about fear. Perhaps your ambition involves an element of danger. If so, it is likely that your close family and friends will be anxious for your safety or the risk of you not returning at all. Again, this has to be planned for. Living with danger is something that people have to overcome. You have to overcome your own fear as well as supporting others. This is where the nature of any supporting relationship is so important. If you are setting yourself personal challenges, you want someone who understands the risks but who can live with reality.

People often look at those who have achieved an ambition as if they are blessed with some kind of special gift. In reality, those who do succeed usually do so because they have a different attitude. They really do have a 'can do' philosophy which enables them to keep going when other people would flag, or start when others are still prevaricating. How do you gain this attitude? The first question must be: do you want to change your attitude? If the answer if yes, you need to employ a number of key behaviours.

It is almost like throwing a switch which turns negative behaviour into positive. The pursuit of ambition can be tiring, which is why it is essential to build in times and ways of recharging your batteries. The difficulty can be in knowing when to do this. There is a variety of ways of planning it. One method is to go through the 12-month calendar and build in breaks at regular intervals, say every six to eight weeks. That way you build events and other activities around these set times. An alternative is to tune in to your body and disappear to take breaks when you feel you need a change of scenery or a rest. There are downsides to both: the first approach may be too structured and you may not be able to go when you plan; the second has the inbuilt danger of leaving it too late, with you keeling over before you recognise the symptoms. In reality, the most sensible route is to recognise the need for breaks and then to respond to your physical well-being and other constraints by timetabling ad hoc breaks.

Change of pace

During these breaks, think about how to make the best use of time. Initially, you may feel the need just to catch up on sleep or to stare into space. However, you will probably find that you will feel much better if you do some form of physical activity or go somewhere completely different. Many people who have fulfilled their potential go away and have favourite places to go to recharge.

Walk tall!

It would be foolish to pretend that fulfilling an ambition is easy; after all, if it were that easy where would the challenge be? However, once you have identified your ambition you have a different focus. You can still be committed to work, family and friends, but you will be nurturing something special, like a jewel glowing in the recesses of your mind. The achievement of a team challenge can create a bond so strong that it lasts for ever. It is a different motivation, which generates a special feeling of warmth – a pride and a hope of things to come – and a fondness of things remembered.

Taking time out to indulge your creativity sparkles; it beckons; you need to sustain it through the hard times, when you become tired or distracted and you doubt your commitment, but ultimately if you keep going you will reach a level of personal satisfaction which you have only dreamt about.

Enriching my life

How I enrich my life is about:

- identifying my strengths and development areas;
- deciding what I want to do in the future;
- inviting others to give me feedback;
- developing independence and confidence;
- delegating responsibility;
- nourishing my talent;
- taking intelligent risks;
- setting realistic and attainable goals.

Ask yourself the following questions:

- What do I know about me which could impact on the way I develop myself?
- Who can help me develop more insight?
- How could I modify, change or develop my behaviour in order to grow?
- How could I think creatively about my development?
- What innovation could I introduce in the way I develop myself?
- How could self-development make a difference to me?
- How could I use coaching to help me?
- How can I ask questions which help me to develop?
- Do I have a strong sense of my own self-worth and capabilities?
- How resilient am I? How willing am I to accept feedback and really respond positively to it?
- How easy do I find it to switch off? How often do I take time to socialise with others informally both in and out of work?
- Do I seek to broaden my perspective by taking time to mix with people with different interests or backgrounds, or people who may challenge me?
- Do I have a network of people who can stimulate, energise and support me?

Finally, the following quote illustrates the fundamental point in this chapter:

Most people give up just when they're about to achieve success. They quit on the one yard line. They give up at the last minute of the game one-foot from a winning touch.

(H. Ross Perot, in Exley, *The Best of Business Quotations*, 1993)

12 Resources and other sources of inspiration

This chapter contains reference to a range of websites which underpin the development of a cross-curricular approach to creativity. It is by no means complete; new sites are coming online every day. Many of the websites have links to other resources. While I have tried to ensure that each link is still 'live', sites close or change names all the time. Equally, the listing does not imply that the sites express the views of the author.

In addition, at the end of this chapter I have tried to draw the key themes of this book together with some questions that you might want to consider in relation to the approach to creativity within your organisation.

I hope you enjoyed reading this book and that in some small way it contributes to the ongoing debate about creativity. Above all, I hope that the increasing emphasis on creativity means that every child entering school has the opportunity to fulfil their creative potential. If you would like to contact me, I can be contacted through the following email: contact@theinspirationnetwork.co.uk. I am also in the process of establishing a new website called www.inspiringkidz.com. Inspiring Kidz is a one-stop guide to inspiring children. It is about giving all children the opportunity to fulfil their potential. It is a directory designed for parents and teachers, a place to share ideas, best practice teaching and to identify sources of materials that inspire, excite and stimulate creative approaches to learning. If you would like to be listed please contact me as above.

Museums, art galleries, theatres, libraries

www.museums.co.uk
www.24hourmuseum.org.uk
http://northvalley.net/kids/museums.shtml
www.mnsu.edu/emuseum/archaeology/museums/
www.cultureonline.gov.uk/
www.officiallondontheatre.co.uk/kids/teachers
http://www.thebritishmuseum.ac.uk/education/onlinelearning/
   home.html
www.britisharts.co.uk/
www.russell-cotes.bournemouth.gov.uk
www.museumofcostume.co.uk
www.londontourist.org/art.html
www.nmm.ac.uk
www.nmmc.co.uk
http://icom.museum/vlmp/galleries.html
www.tate.org.uk/
www.royalacademy.org.uk/
www.rfh.org.uk
http://arts.guardian.co.uk
www.bl.uk/

General interest/cross-curriculum

www.edenproject.com
www.curriculumonline.gov.uk
www.schoolzone.co.uk
www.globaldimension.org.uk/
www.ase.org.uk/
http://www.schoolhistory.co.uk/
www.wiredforhealth.gov.uk/
www.byteachers.org.uk/
www.teachit.co.uk/
www.sln.org.uk/geography/
www.geography-site.co.uk/
www.wwflearning.org.uk/wwflearning-home/
www.ltscotland.org.uk/

www.vso.org.uk/
www.theteachernet.co.uk/
www.bbc.co.uk/schools/
www.bbc.co.uk/schools/gcsebitesize/
www.afpe.org.uk/
www.countrysideaccess.gov.uk/
www.oxfam.org.uk
www.realfrench.net/
http://amazing-space.stsci.edu/
www.worldaware.org.uk/
www.learningcurve.gov.uk/howto/teacherlinks.htm
www.abrsm.org
www.recyclezone.org.uk
www.english-nature.org.uk/science/nature_for_schools
www.spl.org.uk/youngpeople/education/links.htm
www.discoveringpoetry.co.uk/
www.britishcouncil.org/arts-literature.htm
www.creativedrama.com/
www.rnli.org.uk/
www.inspiringkidz.com

Gifted children

www.nagty.ac.uk

Creativity and technology

www.apple.com/education/whyapple/
www.bbc.co.uk/blast/
www.cilt.org.uk/
http://www.microsoft.com/uk/education/skills-dev/innovative-
    teachers/
www.naace.org/
www.becta.org.uk
www.filmeducation.org/
www.icteachers.co.uk/teachers/links/tschools.htm
www.teach-ict.com/
www.nwnet.org.uk/

http://education.smarttech.com
www.bfi.org.uk/

Creative resources for teachers

www.kidsmart.org.uk/teachers/
www.literacytrust.org.uk/
www.primaryresources.co.uk/
www.creativeteachingsite.com
www.classroom-resources.co.uk/
www.alteredbookartists.com
www.teachingideas.co.uk/
www.creativity-portal.com
www.innovationtools.com
www.Edwdebono.com
www.bbc.co.uk/cbbc/
www.peterhoney.com
www.maninthemoon.co.uk
www.learnthings.co.uk
www.coe.uga.edu/torrance/
www.mind-mapping.co.uk/
www.johnseymour-nlp.co.uk

Entrepreneurship

Durham University Business School: Centre for Entrepreneurship,
    www.dur.ac.uk/dbs/faculty/economics_and_finance/
    centre_entrepreneurship/
The Arts Institute in Bournemouth Enterprise Pavilion,
    email: mdesmier@aib.ac.uk
www.writhlingtonorchidproject.org.uk
www.young-enterprise.org.uk/
www.sbs.gov.uk/sbsgov/action/home
www.businesslink.gov.uk
www.dti.gov.uk/
www.ncge.org.uk/

General education

www.dfes.gov.uk/
www.qca.org.uk
www.ncsl.org.uk/
www.ssatrust.org.uk/
www.creative-partnerships.com/
www.gtce.org.uk
www.nc.uk.net
www.ofsted.gov.uk/
www.teachernet.gov.uk/wholeschool/sen/
www.tda.gov.uk
www.talkingteaching.co.uk/
www.basic-skills.co.uk
www.cre.gov.uk/
www.eoc.org.uk/
www.gtcw.org.uk/
www.gtcni.org.uk/
www.gtcs.org.uk
www.globalgateway.org.uk/
www.icg-uk.org/
www.lsc.gov.uk/
www.nsead.org
www.rsa.org.uk
www.hanoverfoundation.org.uk
www.nfer.ac.uk
www.nasen.org.uk
www.youngminds.org.uk

Newspapers, journals

www.tes.co.uk
http://education.guardian.co.uk
www.fastcompany.com
www.tmag.co.uk

Reflections on essential creativity

Based on the content of the earlier chapters, here are some questions that you might want to consider:

1 Do we really understand the full potential of creativity within the curriculum? If not, where can we find out more?
2 Have we made contact with all external sources of 'official' information about creativity?
3 Who really champions creativity within our school or college?
4 Do we design our learning experiences to take account of the different learning styles and multiple intelligences of our learners?
5 As well as traditional methods of teaching, do we also use coaching in the classroom?
6 Have we identified our gifted children or students? Do we give them the opportunity to work with other gifted children? Do we seek external support for them? How well have we integrated them into our school? Do we recognise their giftedness?
7 What could we do to make our school or college environment more inclusive, stimulating and creative for all our learners?
8 Do we actively provide opportunities for individuals to build their self-esteem?
9 Do we have a progressive approach to using technology and blended learning in our creative learning solutions?
10 Have we networked locally to identify creative workers who are prepared to share their knowledge with our school or college?
11 Do we know the full scale of talent in the parents and families of our students?
12 How could we share our creative ideas with our local community?
13 What could we do to develop a spirit of enterprise in our students?
14 Do we spend time working on cross-curricular creative projects?
15 Are we committed to developing our own creativity?
16 Do we share best practice with other schools, colleges and the education marketplace?

Recommended reading

Bennis, W. and Biedermann, P.W. (1997) *Organizing Genius*, Nicholas Brealey, London

Bolles, Richard Nelson (2006) *What Color Is Your Parachute?*, Ten Speed Press, Berkeley, CA

Breen, Bill (2000) 'Where Are You on the Talent Map?', *Fast Company*, 31 December

Brown, Phillip and Hesketh, Anthony (2004) *The Mismanagement of Talent*, Oxford University Press, Oxford

Buckingham, M. (2005) *The One Thing You Need to Know*, Simon & Schuster, London

Butler, P. *et al.* (1997) 'A Revolution in Interaction', *McKinsey Quarterly*, No. 1: 8.

Buzan, Tony (2001) *Head Strong*, Thorsons, London

Cameron, J. (1995) *The Artist's Way*, Pan, Basingstoke and Oxford

Cameron, J. (2002) *Walking in this World*, Rider, London

Crouch, Nigel (2000) *Innovation: The Key to Competitive Advantage*, Director's Guide IOD, 3M and Kogan Page, London

Csikszentmihalyi, Mihaly (1990) *Flow*, Harper & Row, London

Davenport, Thomas H. (2005) *Thinking for a Living: How to Get Better Performance and Results from Knowledge Workers*, Harvard Business School Press, Boston, MA

Dyson, J. (1998) *Against the Odds: An Autobiography*, Trafalgar Square, North Pomfret, VT

Edvinsson, L. and Malone, Michael S. (1997) *Intellectual Capital*, Piatkus, London

Eikleberry, Carol (1999) *The Career Guide for Creative and Unconventional People*, Ten Speed Press, Berkeley, CA

Fowler, H.W. and Fowler, F.G. (1995) *Concise Oxford Dictionary*, 9th edn, Oxford University Press, Oxford

Gardner, Howard (1993) *Frames of Mind*, Basic Books, New York

Gardner, Howard (1997) *Extraordinary Minds*, Phoenix, London

Gelb, Michael (1998) *How to Think like Leonardo da Vinci*, Thorsons, London

Gilbert, I. (2002) *Essential Motivation in the Classroom*, RoutledgeFalmer, London

Goleman, Daniel (1998) *Working with Emotional Intelligence*, Bloomsbury, London

Goleman, Daniel, Boyatzis, Richard and McKee, Annie (2002) *The New Leaders*, Little, Brown, London

Ghoshal, S. and Bartlett, C. (1997) *The Individualized Corporation*, Random House, London

Gregory, Danny (2006) *The Creative License*, Hyperion, New York

Gross, Miraca U.M. (2004) *Exceptionally Gifted Children*, Routledge-Falmer, London

Helmstetter, Shad (1998) *What to Say when You Talk to Yourself*, Thorsons, London

Jeffery, Bob and Woods, Peter (2003) *The Creative School*, Routledge-Falmer, London

Kao, John (1996) *Jamming: The Art and Discipline of Business Creativity*, HarperCollins, London

McNally, David (1993) *Even Eagles Need a Push*, Thorsons, London

Manville, Brook and Foote, Nathaniel (1996) 'Strategy as if Knowledge Mattered', *Fast Company*, April

Michaels, E., Handfield Jones, H. and Axelrod, B. (2001) *The War for Talent*, Harvard Business School Press, Boston, MA

O'Connor, Joseph and Seymour, John (1990) *Introducing NLP: Neuro Linguistic Programming*, Mandala, London

O'Reilly, C.A. and Pfeffer, J. (2000) *Hidden Value: How Great Companies Achieve Extraordinary Results with Ordinary People*, Harvard University Press, Boston, MA

Peters, Tom (1997) *The Circle of Innovation*, Hodder & Stoughton, London

Peters, Tom (1997) 'The Brand Called You', *Fast Company*, August

Ridderstråle, J. and Nordstrom, K. (2000) *Funky Business*, ft.com, London

Rowe, S. and Humphries, S. (2001) 'Creating a Climate for Learning', in A. Craft, B. Jeffrey and M. Liebling (eds), *Creativity in Education*, Continuum, London

Semler, Ricardo (1993) *Maverick*, Arrow, London

Senge, Peter M. (1990) *The Fifth Discipline*, Doubleday, New York

Senge, P., Scharmer, O., Jaworski, J. and Flowers, B. (2004) *Presence*, Nicholas Brealey, London

Sutton, Robert I. (2001) *Weird Ideas that Work*, Free Press, London

Thorne, Kaye (2003) *Managing the Mavericks*, Spiro Publishing, London

Thorne, Kaye (2004) *Coaching for Change*, Kogan Page, London

Thorne, Kaye (2004) *Employer Branding*, Personnel Today Management Resources, Reed Publishing, Surrey

Torrance, E. Paul (1962) *Guiding Creative Talent*, Prentice Hall, Upper Saddle River, NJ

Torrance, E. Paul (2002) *Manifesto: A Guide to Developing a Creative Career*, Ablex, Westport, CT

Tracy, Brian (1993) *Maximum Achievement*, Simon & Schuster, New York

Ulrich, D. and Brockbank, W. (2005) *The HR Value Proposition*, Harvard Business School Press, Boston, MA

US Bureau of Labour Statistics (1999) 'Labour Force 2008', *Monthly Labour Review*, November

Whitmore, J. (1996) *Coaching for Performance*, Nicholas Brealey, London

Winner, Ellen (1997) *Gifted Children*, Basic Books, New York

Please note that copies of my book *Managing the Mavericks* are now only available from The Inspiration Network, www.theinspirationnetwork.co.uk

References

Bolles, Richard Nelson (2006) *What Color Is Your Parachute?*, Ten Speed Press, Berkeley, CA

Brown, Phillip and Hesketh, Anthony (2004) *The Mismanagement of Talent*, Oxford University Press, Oxford

Buzan, Tony (2001) *Head Strong*, Thorsons, London

Cameron, J. (1995) *The Artist's Way*, Pan, Basingstoke and Oxford

Cameron, J. (2002) *Walking in this World*, Rider, London

Crouch, Nigel (2000) *Innovation: The Key to Competitive Advantage*, Director's Guide IOD, 3M and Kogan Page, London

Csikszentmihalyi, Mihaly (1990) *Flow*, Harper & Row, London

Eikleberry, Carol (1999) *The Career Guide for Creative and Unconventional People*, Ten Speed Press, Berkeley, CA

Exley, Helen (1993) *The Best of Business Quotations*, Helen Exley Giftbooks, Watford, Herts

Fishman, Charles (1998) 'The War for Talent', *Fast Company*, 31 July

Fowler, H.W. and Fowler, F.G. (1995) *Concise Oxford Dictionary*, 9th edn, Oxford University Press, Oxford

Gardner, Howard (1993) *Frames of Mind*, Basic Books, New York

Gardner, Howard (1997) *Extraordinary Minds*, Phoenix, London

Gelb, Michael (1998) *How to Think like Leonardo da Vinci*, Thorsons, London

Ghoshal, S. and Bartlett, C. (1997) *The Individualized Corporation*, Random House, London

Gilbert, I. (2002) *Essential Motivation in the Classroom*, RoutledgeFalmer, London

Goleman, Daniel (1998) *Working with Emotional Intelligence*, Bloomsbury, London

Goleman, Daniel, Boyatzis, Richard and McKee, Annie (2002) *The New Leaders*, Little, Brown, London

Gregory, Danny (2006) *The Creative License*, Hyperion, New York

Gross, Miraca U.M. (2004) *Exceptionally Gifted Children*, Routledge-Falmer, London

Helmstetter, Shad (1998) *What to Say when You Talk to Yourself*, Thorsons, London

Jeffery, Bob and Woods, Peter (2003) *The Creative School*, Routledge-Falmer, London

Michaels, E., Handfield Jones, H. and Axelrod, B. (2001) *The War for Talent*, Harvard Business School Press, Boston, MA

Peters, Tom (1997) *The Circle of Innovation*, Hodder & Stoughton, London

Peters, Tom (1997) 'The Brand Called You', *Fast Company*, August

Ridderstråle, J. and Nordstrom, K. (2000) *Funky Business*, ft.com, London

Senge, Peter M. (1990) *The Fifth Discipline*, Doubleday, New York

Sutton, Robert I. (2001) *Weird Ideas that Work*, Free Press, London

Thorne, Kaye (2003) *Managing the Mavericks*, Spiro Publishing, London

Thorne, Kaye (2004) *Employer Branding*, Personnel Today Management Resources, Reed Publishing, Surrey

Torrance, E. Paul (1962) *Guiding Creative Talent*, Prentice Hall, Upper Saddle River, NJ

Torrance, E. Paul (2002) *Manifesto: A Guide to Developing a Creative Career*, Ablex, Westport, CT

Tracy, Brian (1993) *Maximum Achievement*, Simon & Schuster, New York

Whitmore, J. (1996) *Coaching for Performance*, Nicholas Brealey, London

Winner, Ellen (1997) *Gifted Children*, Basic Books, New York

Index